The Binding Force of Tradition

Fr. Chad Ripperger, Ph.D.

Dedicated in Honor of Our Lady of Sorrows,
Who Having Watched Her Son's Passion,
Now Watches over the Passion of His Mystical Body
and is the Remedy for Its Restoration

Table of Contents

Abbreviations

The following abbreviations are used in this text along with those abbreviations in use in standard English. Texts of Saint Thomas:

De Ver.	*Quaestiones Disputatae de Veritate*
Sent.	*In Quatuor Libros Sententiarum*[1]
SCG	*Summa Contra Gentiles*
ST	*Summa Theologiae*

Other texts:

CCC	*Catechism of the Catholic Church*
OCE	*Catholic Encyclopedia*
CED	*Catholic Encyclopedia Dictionary*
CIC/83	*Codex Iuris Canonici*
SSP	*Summary of Scholastic Principles*[2]

---

[1]Citations from the *Sentences* contain first the book number, then the abbreviation, followed by location within the book.

[2]Loyola University, 1951.

Foreword

When Father Ripperger asked me if I would be willing to write the Forward to *The Binding Force of Tradition*, it afforded me the opportunity to pay an exceptional gifted philosopher and theologian a debt of gratitude. During my tenure as Editor of *The Latin Mass* magazine, Father Ripperger penned and permitted me to publish some of the most remarkably insightful essays which argue eloquently for the inherent and unique ability of the ancient Latin Mass to protect and promulgate the fullness of the Catholic Faith. The present work is a much needed corollary to the aforementioned premise which he has so consistently and fluently articulated.

The present work commences with the first intellectual salvo hurled against the Catholic concept of Sacred Tradition just prior to the Second Vatican Council. A circle of European Catholic academicians had been embracing a radical alteration in the Church's theological method. They proposed that Scripture *alone* would henceforth be the standard by which the truths of the Faith were evaluated. They essentially advocated that the four century conflict between Catholicism and Protestantism on this critical point of Christianity's self-reference was to be settled in favor of those claiming the pedigree of Luther.

Anyone familiar with Father Ripperger's overall analysis of the roots of the current crisis in the Church is very much aware that he views immanentism as the primary viral agent assaulting (with increasing intensity) the health of the Mystical Body. Though he does not analyze the issue under discussion from this perspective, it is of more than passing interest to note that immanentist presuppositions were central to the thinking of those Catholic theologians advocating a revolution in the Church's understanding of Revelation.

Father Ripperger early in this present work documents that Dominican Father Yves Congar, one of the most influential *periti* at the Second Vatican Council, was among the most seminal figures advocating a role adjustment in the relationship between Sacred Tradition and Sacred Scripture. In a work published after the Council (*The Word and the Spirit*), he pithily summarizes the essential error within the writings of two Catholic Scripture scholars and the reasons why they were condemned:

> Since the decree *Lamentabili* of July 3, 1907, the Catholic treatises on Revelation included a paragraph about how Revelation closed with the death of the last Apostle. The condemned proposition was formulated as follows: "Revelation, which constitutes the object of the Catholic Faith, was not completed with the Apostles." The target of this condemnation was a concept of Revelation which, like that proposed

by Loisy, considered <u>Revelation to be the religious intuitions of mankind</u>, a perception that broadens and becomes more perfect in relations between man and the unknown God. <u>Or the mystical view of Tyrrell for whom Revelation relies on an interior act, an appeal or prophetic message that continues to appear in the religious consciences [of men]</u>. Tyrrell admitted, however, that "the revelation given by Christ and the Apostles, independent of further theological reflection, already contained everything necessary for the fullness of the life of faith, hope, and charity. With the death of the last Apostle, the regulatory, classical period of Christian inspiration closed. Not in the sense that revelation - which is to a certain degree the privilege of each man - would have ceased abruptly, but in the sense that every further revelation needs to be controlled and checked in accordance with apostolic revelation." [Emphases mine]

Thus, the heretical views of Fathers Loisy and Tyrrell regarding Revelation can be seen, at their core, to reflect the immanentist mind set. Despite Pius X's condemnations, a related development was occurring among many of the Catholic biblical theologians which would, effectively, incorporate immanentist notions into the study of Holy Scripture.

Since the mid-20th century there had been a quiet but deliberate stampede of Catholic Scripturists toward the Protestant exegetical method which had divested the Scriptures of the assumption of their historicity. The Gospels, especially, were increasingly addressed as documents produced by a "faith community" of early Christians whose "traditions" concerning Christ had been developed under diverse influences and personalities. From a historical account of what Our Lord really said and did, the Gospels became an historical legacy of what particular groups within the primitive Church *believed* He said and did. Contemporary Christians, according to this view, must be faithful to this heritage by viewing the Scriptures through the prism of their own cultures and experiences and both interpret them and apply them accordingly. So, in the end, what is supposed to be a fixed external measurement of doctrine and dogma is transformed into an internal process of a subjective methodology and the Person and message of Christ becomes nothing more than a multi cultural self reflection emanating from within a historical mirror into which the Church of any given epoch peers.

Sacred Tradition essentially is the Church's Magisterium, throughout history, fleshing out the Divine Revelation which ended with the death of the last Apostle. As the complementary font of Divine Revelation, it is intertwined with Sacred Scripture and assumes the latter's historicity. If the same immanentist methodology of interpretation and application becomes the norm for Sacred Tradition, "living tradition" will acquire an entirely novel definition and God will be relegated to being the Creator who emulates His creatures.

Father Ripperger utilizes the exacting scalpel of Thomistic precision to explain the problem and its solution. As much as this work comes under the rubric of a theological treatise, it is more than that in terms of its potential to affect the everyday Catholic. Many of you are aware of Father Ripperger's magnum opus, *Introduction to the Science of Mental Health*. Demonstrating the utility of St. Thomas to acquire a robust and accurate understanding of human nature, this three volume work offers a comprehensive analysis of objective human nature as the Creator intended it to be; at the same time it offers a sober estimate of the vicissitudes of a wounded human nature as it struggles to fulfill its purpose as designed by its Maker. One of the major obstacles to righting fallen human nature is the bane of contradiction. For Catholics struggling to order their intellects to the One True Faith in these times when all is in flux, *The Binding Force of Tradition* lifts the fog of confusion over a question which involves the heart of Catholicity, and sweeps clean the faddish debris of contemporary clutter.

Father James McLucas

Introduction

Very often those who attend the ancient rite of Mass and who have a love for all aspects of the Sacred Tradition of the Roman Catholic Church are often told that this is merely a matter of preference in relationship to everything that has come to us since the Second Vatican Council. In this respect, the modernists adhere faithfully to their principle that the subjective dispositions of the individual are to remain sacrosanct as well as respected. In their mind, if this simply means that there are some who like the old forms and the old teachings, that is to be respected as long as those who adhere to those old forms and teachings accepts the full validity of what has come since the Second Vatican Council.

However, those who adhere to the Sacred Tradition find it alarming that the tradition is very often dismissed with a slight of hand or just simply ignored as if it had no import, binding force or relevance. Those who adhere to the Sacred Tradition very often have a vague understanding or impression that the tradition is something more than a preference. Rooted in their *Sensus Fidelium* is something telling them that it is even more than just a recognition and love of the good and the beauty of those things that are passed on to us through the Sacred Tradition. It is much more than that. In this humble and inadequate work, it is my hope that it will contribute to a serious recognition that the Sacred Tradition is something binding on all of us for a variety of different reasons.

Chapter 1: The Rule of Faith

When the word "tradition" is brought up in the context of a theological discussion, one receives three different kinds of reactions in relationship to the word or concept. The first is a simple dismissal in the sense that tradition does not bind in any way based upon the assertion that theological notions are constantly changing. Since they are constantly changing, "newer" is always better and the tradition has no binding force on the level of moral obligation because it is not "newer." Broadly, we may label this the liberal position. The second is in connection to what is called notional assent. Notional assent is an intellectual judgment that a particular proposition is true but in the practical living of a person's life, it is not followed. This is seen when the Magisterium promulgates that the tradition is part of divine revelation even after Vatican II,[3] but will promulgate documents that have no connection or reference to any document on the same subject prior to the Second Vatican Council.[4] Even certain neo-conservatives, or what are sometimes called neo-Catholics, suffer from this. The third is based on what is called real assent. Real assent is an intellectual judgment that a particular proposition is true *and* the person leads his life according to it. Those Catholics who follow the orthodox traditional teaching as manifested in the Fathers and doctors of the Church fall into this category insofar as they hold to the actual value and binding force of the tradition and lead their life according to it as well.[5] The purpose of this section of our work will be to explicate the various reasons why we are bound morally to follow the Sacred Tradition of the Catholic Church.

I. The Rule of Faith

Any time one is bound to do something morally, it is based upon a particular precept or, we may say, *regula* or rule which we must follow. The question then becomes: what is this rule or standard which we must adhere to morally in relationship to the tradition? Some modern discussions of the

---

[3]See *Catechism of the Catholic Church*, para. 75-83.

[4]For example, compare the document of Vatican II on ecumenism, *Unitatis Redintegratio, Ut Unum Sint* by Pope John Paul II, *Satis Cognitum* by Leo XIII and *Mortalium Animos* by Pius XI.

[5]It should be noted that some of those who call themselves traditionalists today do not follow the tradition fully and therefore give only notional assent to part of it.

rule of faith leave the average orthodox Catholic a bit concerned. For example, one reads in the work *The Meaning of Tradition* by Yves Congar this startling passage:

> I have analyzed elsewhere the process by which a number of theologians have come to identify tradition with the teaching of the Magisterium. During the difficult period of the Modernist crisis, Fr. L. Billot expounded this theology in the most emphatic way by criticizing historicism. He reproached those who distinguished the Magisterium from tradition, and who claimed the latter as at least approaching a rule of faith, with confusing *object* and *rule*. According to him, tradition was indeed the object of faith, but it was the rule of faith in the act by which the Magisterium transmitted this object with authority, with the result that the rule of faith was really the preaching or active tradition of the Magisterium. Fr. L. Billot's position by no means compels recognition.[6]

This text is problematic since it seems to indicate that what we are to believe, i.e. the rule of faith, is not the Magisterium. In the current historical context, such a proposition would appear to play into the hands of many heterodox theologians who assert that we are not bound by what the Magisterium says.

The then Father (later to be Cardinal) Congar wrote this text just before and during the Second Vatican Council. The import of this is obvious: it was written during the time in which the preparatory work of the Second Vatican Council was being done and while the council itself was discussing the document *Dei Verbum*, which treats of revelation and the Magisterium. Throughout the text of *The Meaning of Tradition*, he asserts that THE rule of faith is not the Magisterium but Scripture. This thesis is also the theme of his technical work on tradition, entitled in English *Tradition and Traditions*,[7] of which we shall give some analysis. This thesis becomes even more important when we consider the backdrop of Vatican II and the fact that Congar exerted significant influence over the text of the schema *Dei Verbum*.[8]

Yet we should not be too quick to dismiss Cardinal Congar's thesis,

---

[6] Congar, *Meaning of Tradition*, p. 69.

[7] Congar, *Tradition and Traditions*. The French original was entitled *La Tradition et les Traditions*. Notations in this text will be from the English translation.

[8] Avery Cardinal Dulles wrote: "And, as Joseph Ratzinger has observed, it is 'not difficult...to recognize the pen of Y. Congar' in the ideas and the language of the text." Taken from the Foreword in Congar, *Meaning of Tradition*, p. viii.

insofar as the discussion of what the rule of faith actually is manifests different theories of what actually is the rule of faith. Therefore, in relation to the rule of faith, we shall consider four things. The first is what is meant by the term "rule of faith." Second, a consideration will be given to the various usages of that term historically. Third, we shall see if the various theories are in any way reconcilable, and fourth, we shall discuss what happens when members of the Magisterium are discordant from the Rule of Faith.

A. The Term "Rule of Faith."

In the old *Catholic Encyclopedia*, we read the following definition of the rule of faith: "The word *rule* (Lat. *regula*, Gr. *kanon*) means a standard by which something can be tested, and the rule of faith means something extrinsic to our faith, and serving as its norm or measure."[9] The rule of faith is the standard by which one tests what one believes to determine if what one believes is in fact true. St. Thomas tells us in his commentary on Peter Lombard's *Sentences* that "in every moderation, it is necessary that that which is moderated is adequated to some rule or measure."[10] A rule is something to which our knowledge is adequated. Of course the term "adequation" is the foundational term in the definition of truth: *adaequatio intellectus et rei*[11] (adequation of intellect and thing). In the case of the rule of faith, our intellect must conform to the rule in order for our faith to be true. What is at the root of the entire discussion is orthodoxy, since the term "orthodoxy" comes from the Greek terms *orthos* and *doxis*, which mean right belief. We believe rightly, i.e. we are orthodox, when our belief conforms to the rule of faith.

St. Thomas often uses the term rule or measure in relation to actions as they conform to the law which is the rule.[12] The phrase *lex credendi lex orandi* is sometimes translated as "the rule of believing determines the rule of praying." By deduction then we see that the right kind of worship is determined by what we believe, i.e. ultimately, the rule of faith. Establishing precisely what constitutes the rule of faith is important.

---

[9] OCE, vol. V, p. 766.

[10] III Sent., d. 33, q. 3, a. 4a: "in omni autem moderationem, oportet quod illud quod moderatur, mensurae sive regulae alicui adaequetur." See also, ST I-II, q. 64, a. 1 and a. 3.

[11] De ver., q. 1, a. 1.

[12] See ST I-II, q.; 90, a. 4; ibid., q. 91, a. 2 and *Super I ad Cor.* I, l. 7, c. 2.

II. The Different Historical Usages of the Term "Rule of Faith"

A. God as the Rule

St. Thomas says that among those things which rule others, there is something which rules but in no way is ruled and this is the notion of the first rule and such is God.[13] In the *Prima Secundae* of the *Summa Theologiae*, we read:

> Measure is able to be taken in two ways in relation to theological virtue. One indeed is according to the very notion of the virtue and so the measure and rule of theological virtue is God Himself. For our faith is regulated according to the divine truth; charity according to His goodness; hope, moreover, according to the magnitude of His omnipotence and piety.[14]

The first rule of faith above all others is God Himself and as God reveals Himself that knowledge becomes the divine truth to which we must adhere.

Yet, since we are trying to get to THE rule of faith, we must first not only define rule, as we have, but we must also define faith. Each virtue inclines us to act and so the virtue of faith inclines us to the act of assent to that which is believed,[15] since to give assent is the act of faith.[16] Assent is an act of the intellect in which the intellect sees or adheres to some proposition as true.[17] So, we may define faith as a virtue (habit) residing in the possible

---

[13]III Sent., d. 25, q. 2, a. 1d, ad 2: "ita etiam est in regulantibus, quod est aliquid quod est regulans et nullo modo regulatum; et haec est ratio primae regulae, et tale est Deus."

[14]ST I-II, q. 64, a. 4: "Virtutis autem theologicae duplex potest accipi mensura. Una quidem secundum ipsam rationem virtutis. Et sic mensura et regula virtutis theologicae est ipse Deus, fides enim nostra regulatur secundum veritatem divinam, caritas autem secundum bonitatem eius, spes autem secundum magnitudinem omnipotentiae et pietatis eius." See also ST II-II, q. 2, a. 6, ad 3 and ibid., q. 17, a. 5, ad 2.

[15]ST II-II, q. 1, a. 4. This discussion on the nature of the virtue of faith is taken in substance from Ripperger, *Introduction to the Science of Mental Health*, vol. II, p. 52f.

[16]ST II-II, q. 2, a. 1.

[17]See Attwater, *A Catholic Dictionary*, p. 40.

intellect (the subject[18] of the habit or virtue) by which one gives assent (act of virtue)[19] to those things revealed by God (object of virtue, sometimes called the Deposit of Faith). This definition of faith does not differ in substance from the two definitions which St. Thomas gives of faith. The first is *substantia sperandarum rerum, argumentum non apparentium*[20] (the substance of things hoped for, the evidence of things unseen). In this definition, faith refers to the things in which one must believe, i.e. those things revealed by God and to this is given the phrase *the substance of things hoped for*, for God[21] and eternal beatitude are those things revealed and hoped for. The evidence (*argumentum*) of things not seen refers to two things, the first is to the faith which moves the intellect as if by argument,[22] if you will, to see the truth of what is revealed. The second refers to the things unseen, since eternal beatitude, God, etc. are things which are unseen.[23] The other definition of faith given by St. Thomas is: *habitus mentis, qua inchoatur vita eterna in nobis, faciens intellectum assentire non apparentibus* (a habit of the mind, by which eternal life is begun in us, making the intellect assent to things unseen). In this definition, we find the same elements in the other definition, viz. faith is a virtue or habit in the intellect by which we give assent to things that are non-apparent or unseen. But this definition also indicates that faith is the beginning of eternal life. Since faith is necessary to order us to God in a sufficient manner[24] and since eternal beatitude consists in seeing God face to

---

[18]That faith is in the intellect as in a subject, see ST II-II, q. 4, a. 2 and De ver., q. 14, a. 4.

[19]This act of belief is in the second act of the intellect of judgment, see De ver., q. 14, a. 1.

[20]De ver., q. 14, a. 2 (taken from Hebrews 11:1).

[21]ST II-II, q. 4, a. 1.

[22]Here "argument" is used in the philosophical sense as "1. A reason or reasons for or against (a proposition, thesis, hypothesis, opinion, action, etc). 2. The process of finding, presenting or organizing reason for or against something." In effect, the virtue of faith makes the propositions or articles of faith believable since one can see the truth of the propositions by faith. For this reason, St. Thomas observes that the term *argumentum* indicates conviction which means that one holds firmly to the truth of the thing, or literally overcome with (*cum vincere*) the truth of the proposition. See De ver., q. 14, a. 2.

[23]ST II-II, q. II-II, q. 1, a. 4 and De ver., q. 14, a. 2.

[24]ST I-II, q. 62, a. 1, ad 3.

face, then faith is the beginning by which we start striving for perfect beatitude.

Therefore, from the definition of rule and the definition of faith, we see that THE rule of faith is God, i.e. the divine truth which God has revealed about Himself. This definition of faith and rule determines the subsequent discussion of the other rules of faith. Since God is THE rule of faith, then any other rule will simply be *a* rule of faith in relation to the first rule. Yet, the OCE observes that:

> Since faith is Divine and infallible, the rule of faith must be also Divine and infallible; and since faith is supernatural assent to Divine truths upon Divine authority, the ultimate or remote rule of faith must be the truthfulness of God in revealing Himself. But since Divine revelation is contained in the written books and unwritten traditions (Vatican Council, I, ii), the Bible and Divine tradition must be the rule of our faith.[25]

Here we see two things of importance. The first is that while God is THE rule of faith, nevertheless, knowledge about God, which we call revelation, is contained in Scripture and tradition. Second, since God did not reveal to us personally, i.e. He revealed to prophets and to the Apostles and disciples of the New Testament, then God is only the remote rule of faith for us.[26]

B. The Theological Virtue of Faith as the Rule

Since the theological virtue of faith is a virtue infused in the possible intellect by which we give assent to the Deposit of Faith, which are the teachings of God about Himself, the theological virtue of faith becomes a kind of rule. Since every habit is specified by its object,[27] the virtue of faith has God, or the revealed truth about God, as its object. St. Thomas observes that a single heresy corrupts the virtue of faith.[28] Hence, when one considers a proposition which is proposed to be believed, then one knows whether that

---

[25] OCE, loc. cit.

[26] As will be seen, the remote rule is that from which approximate rule derives its teaching.

[27] ST I-II, q. 54, a. 2; ibid., q. 60, a. 1; ibid., q. 63, a. 4 and III Sent., d. 33, q. 1., a. 1., qu. 1.

[28] ST II-II, q. 5, a. 3. Since one cannot be saved without faith, we see how important the rule of faith is for our salvation. Orthodoxy is the only means to salvation. Cf. James 2:10.

11

proposition is true or not if it is the proper object of, or corrupts, the virtue of faith. While ontologically this is true, epistemologically it is difficult for man to know if a specific proposition corrupts his virtue of faith or not, since we do not have an immediate vision of the virtue of faith in us. We know indirectly that we have the virtue of faith insofar as we know that we see the propositions, creedal statements or symbols as true. But here again we have a problem. For someone can say he gives assent to the proposition but he may not understand the same thing by that proposition as the Church understands. For this reason, we are forced to seek a different rule by which we can know whether what we believe is true or not.

C. Revelation
1. Scripture *and* Tradition as the Rule

The OCE asserts that Scripture and tradition are the rule of faith.[29] In considering revelation as the rule, we are drawn to the words of the First Vatican Council:

> This supernatural revelation, according to the faith of the universal Church declared by the holy Council of Trent is contained "in the written books and unwritten traditions which were received by the Apostles from the very mouth of Christ or dictated to the Apostles by the Holy Spirit, as if given by hand, they come to us."[30]

Revelation comes to us by means of Scripture and unwritten traditions or, we may say generically, tradition. We shall return to this discussion of whether the rule is Scripture and tradition or merely Scripture. Here the term "tradition" is being used in its more restrictive sense as referring to those things handed down which are contradistinguished from Scripture and not in the broader sense in which tradition is taken as comprising everything that is

---

[29] Actually the OCE (loc. cit) asserts that they are: "only silent witnesses and cannot interpret themselves, they are commonly termed 'proximate but inanimate rules of faith'. Unless, then, the Bible and tradition are to be profitless, we must look for some proximate rule which shall be animate or living."

[30] Vatican I, *Dei Filius*, c. 2 (Denz. 3006/1787): "Haec porro supernaturalis revelatio, secundum universalis Ecclesiae fidem a sancta Tridentina Synodo declaratam continetur 'in libris scriptis et sine scripto traditionibus, quae ipsius Christi ore ab Apostolis acceptae, aut (ab) ipsis Apostolis Spiritu Sancto dictante quasi per manus traditae, ad nos usque pervenerunt.'" See also Pope. St. Pius X, *Lamentabili*, prop. 20 (Denz. 3421/2020).

passed on, even the Scriptures.[31] John Henry Cardinal Newman asserted that Scripture and tradition are a "two-fold rule" of faith.[32]

2. Doctrine Taught by the Apostles

Tertullian in his work *De Præscriptione Hæreticorum* says that the rule of faith consists in the tradition of the Apostles by which the teaching of the Apostles is passed on. He maintains that it is by the doctrine of the Apostles that one knows that what one holds is true and all other doctrines are false.[33] Thus, "for the ante-Nicene Fathers 'rule of faith', 'rule of truth', designate the doctrine taught by the Church in accordance with what it received from the apostles."[34]

D. The Creed as Rule

Yet, the doctrine of the Apostles which is taught by the Church is contained in Scripture and tradition and one may even say that the doctrine taught by the Apostles is formulated in the Creed. Tertullian in *Adversus Praxean*[35] recites what appears to be a creed and then notes that this is the rule of faith. St. Augustine says it explicitly: "Receive, my children, the Rule of Faith, which is called the Symbol."[36] It is a common practice of the Fathers to write works which contain creedal formulas which are often the guide or "rule" for the other works.[37]

St. Thomas, writing in the Augustinian theological tradition, also

---

[31]This will be discussed later in the book.

[32]John Henry Cardinal Newman, *Certain Difficulties Felt by Anglicans in Catholic Teaching* as quoted by Congar in *Tradition and Traditions*, p. 118.

[33]See Tertullian, *De Præscriptione Hæreticorum*, c. XXI (as found in ANF 3:252).

[34]Congar, *Tradition and Traditions*, p. 27.

[35]Tertullian, *Adversus Praxean*, c. III (as found in ANF 3:598). See also Tertullian, *De Præscriptione Hæreticorum*, c. XIII.

[36]St. Augustine, *De Symbolo ad Catechumenos*, c. I (as found in NPNF 3:369).

[37]See also Congar, *Tradition and Traditions*, p. 29.

affirms that the Creed or Symbols[38] are the rule of faith.[39] He also refers to statements of the Creed as articles, and regarding these articles, he observes that "there are not some natural principles innate in us to which the articles of faith are able to be reduced, but the whole determination of faith is in us by doctrine."[40] The doctrine or teachings which we must believe are not in us innately nor are they in us by infusion of the theological virtue of faith, rather they come to us by teaching. St. Thomas says that the teachings necessary for faith are collected together in the Creed so that they are accessible to all men.[41]

E. Scripture
1. *Sola Scriptura* as the Rule of Faith
　　　　It is commonly known that among some of the Protestants, Scripture alone is the rule. This position with some nuancing has become the position of some modern theologians.[42] Karl Rahner held that "For theology, Scripture is practically the only material source of the faith, to which it must refer as to the source clearly original, not derived and 'norma non normata'."[43] Elsewhere he asserts:

> The Second Vatican Council refused to make tradition a second source for us today which exists by itself alongside scripture, a source which testifies to individual, material contents of faith which have no foundation at all in scripture. However, much the more precise

---

[38]The propositions of the Creed were called "symbols" because the spiritual realities could be symbolized by the words or propositions of the Creed.

[39]See *Compendium Theologiae*, l. 1, cc. 40, 42, 43 and 46-8; *in Symbolum Apostolorum*, a. 7 and *Catena Aurea in Matthaeum*, c. 24, p. 6. In these works, St. Thomas at times refers to the Creed as "regula fidei catholicae" - the rule of Catholic faith.

[40]III Sent., d., 25, q. 2, a. 1d, ad 1: "non sunt nobis innata aliqua principia naturalia ad quae possint reduci articuli fidei; sed tota determinatio fidei est in nobis per doctrinam."

[41]ST II-II, q. 1, a. 9.

[42]Ratzinger in *Revelation and Tradition* (p. 32) asserts that the modern version of the notion that Scripture contains everything revealed began with J.R. Geiselmann's interpretation of Trent. The later pope does not subscribe to this position and even refutes it, see p. 34 and 45f.

[43]Rahner, *Sacra Scrittura e Teologia*, p. 168 as quoted by Cardinal Siri, *Gethsemani: Reflections on the Contemporary Theological Movement*, p. 33.

relationship between scripture and tradition still needs a great deal of further theological clarification; it is perhaps obvious from what has already been said earlier that the 'scripture alone' of the Reformation is no longer a doctrine which distinguishes and separates the churches.[44]

Putting aside the infallible definition of Trent that revelation is in both unwritten traditions and Scripture,[45] it is not the case that the Second Vatican Council refused to make tradition a source.[46] While it is true that "an attempt was made to deny the sources of Revelation saying there was only one Source [i.e. Scripture],"[47] *Dei Verbum* says, "She [the Church] has always maintained them [Scripture], and continues to do so, *together with sacred tradition*, as the supreme rule of faith."[48]

Congar has a more refined approach to the notion that Scripture is the only material source of doctrine and the only rule of faith. While he asserts that Scripture is the rule of faith,[49] he says that Scripture is the rule of faith only "when conjoined to the Church and her tradition."[50] Yet, this must be viewed in relation to his statements elsewhere, where he asserts that

> The holy Scriptures have an absolute value that tradition has not, which is why, without being the absolute rule of every other norm, like the Protestant scriptural principle, they are the supreme guide to

---

[44]Rahner, *Foundations of Christian Faith: An Introduction to the Idea of Christianity*, p. 377f.

[45]See Session 4.

[46]This same factual error was made by Pope Paul VI during a Wednesday audience (March 26th, 1969) when he said, "And the whole of the dogmatic Constitution 'Dei Verbum' is an apologia of the Holy Scriptures, as the supreme rule of faith (n. 21)" (*L'Osservatore Romano*, Weekly Edition in English, 3 April 1969, page 10).

[47]Siri, *Gethsemani*, p. 31.

[48]Para. 21. See also para. 9.

[49]Congar, *Tradition and Traditions*, passim and *Meaning of Tradition*, passim.

[50]Congar, *Tradition and Traditions*, p. 41 and 45.

which any others there may be are subjected.[51]

This statement, as we shall see, is hard to maintain when theological analysis is given to doctrines not contained in Scripture but which are necessary for salvation. Moreover, it is hard to maintain when one considers that ultimately, THE rule is God and Scripture is a means of transmission of the Deposit, not the Deposit itself and therefore the Deposit of Faith would take precedence even over Scripture.

Yet, Congar's thesis that Scripture is "at least the negative norm, of all interpretation and transmission"[52] is true, not as "the" norm but as "a" norm. No theological proposition or doctrine can be considered true if it contradicts Scripture *as understood by the Church.* It is not merely a matter of whether something we think denies some passage in Scripture, but whether it actually denies what the Church understands the particular passage to contain. This would require a Magisterium which would be assisted by the Holy Spirit in knowing the meaning of the passage and not merely leaving it to private interpretation. In this respect, we concur with Cardinal Billot that Scripture can be a *remote* rule.[53]

2. Why Scripture is not THE Rule of Faith
We read in the *Secunda Secundae* of the Summa Theologiae, that

> The truth of the faith is diffusely and in various modes contained in sacred Scripture, and in certain cases obscurely, so that long study and training (*exercitium*) is required to elicit the truth of the faith from sacred Scripture, to which not all are able to come to that which is necessary to know the truth of faith, and which they do not have the leisure to study, being busy with other affairs. And therefore it was necessary that from the passages of sacred Scripture some manifest summary would be gathered together which would be proposed to all to be believed, which indeed is not added to sacred Scripture but

---

[51] Congar, *Meaning of Tradition,* p. 100. In *Tradition and Traditions* (p. 140), he observes: "Luther, of course, early on was very strongly convinced, as a result of his teaching (Trutvetter), of the absolute primacy of Scripture over all other authority, and in that he was completely Catholic."

[52] Ibid., p. 314.

[53] Billot, *De Immutabilitate Traditionis contra Modernam Hæresim Evolutionismi,* p. 23, footnote 1.

16

rather is taken from sacred Scripture.[54]

A rule of faith must be accessible to the general run of men since one must conform to it in order to be saved. Historically, many could not read; many do not have the leisure, i.e. the time, for the study of sacred Scripture, yet everyone can hear the preaching of the Church.[55]

Moreover, some parts of revelation were given to the Apostles and they taught them to the first Christians prior to the writing of the Scriptures. Therefore, there must have been something which was the rule of faith for them prior to the writing of Scripture. In this sense, Scripture cannot be THE rule of faith. Scripture is not necessary for salvation[56] insofar as one might never read a line of Scripture and still be saved, but one cannot depart from the rule of faith and be saved.[57] In fact, history, by the force of Divine Providence, could have been different insofar as God could have chosen never to move the Apostles to write down what was revealed to them. Even in this case, what would have been necessary for salvation would have been passed on from generation to generation due to the infallibility of tradition. Even Congar admits that Scripture is not of the essence of the Church.[58] In fact, establishing the certitude of what is contained in Scripture as well as

---

[54]ST II-II, q. 1, a. 9, ad 1: "veritas fidei in sacra scriptura diffuse continetur et variis modis, et in quibusdam obscure; ita quod ad eliciendum fidei veritatem ex sacra scriptura requiritur longum studium et exercitium, ad quod non possunt pervenire omnes illi quibus necessarium est cognoscere fidei veritatem, quorum plerique, aliis negotiis occupati, studio vacare non possunt. Et ideo fuit necessarium ut ex sententiis sacrae scripturae aliquid manifestum summarie colligeretur quod proponeretur omnibus ad credendum. Quod quidem non est additum sacrae scripturae, sed potius ex sacra scriptura assumptum."

[55]That Scripture is not self-explanatory and even heretics appeal to it, see Congar, *Tradition and Traditions*, p. 382.

[56]See also Gannon, *The Rule of Faith: Scripture and Tradition*, p. 5.

[57]If Scripture was THE rule and therefore necessary for salvation, entire generations, which could not read or have access to the Scriptures which were often rare and expensive, would have been lost. In a sense, it would militate against the Mark of Catholicity of the Church since not all men could have access to salvation.

[58]Congar, *Tradition and Traditions*, p. 285. What is of the essence of the Church is revelation. Scripture constitutes a *means* of transmission of revelation or the Deposit of Faith and is not the Deposit of Faith itself. This is why it is called a "font" of revelation and not revelation itself. Scripture is an instrument used by God and the Church to preserve the teaching of revelation. See Gannon, *The Rule of Faith*, p. 9f.

determining which texts are actually inspired required a Magisterium.[59]

Even the Scriptures themselves indicate that the Scriptures are not enough. St. Paul tells us in his second letter to the Thessalonians (2:14) "Therefore, brethren, stand fast: and hold the traditions, which you have learned, whether by word or by our epistle." Why would we have to hold fast to the traditions by word, i.e orally received, if Scriptures sufficed?[60]

3. Scripture Does not Contain Everything Necessary for Salvation

Scripture cannot be THE rule because it does not contain everything necessary for salvation.[61] Even Congar treats of the doctrines not contained within Scripture.[62] Those doctrines which historically have not been considered to be contained in Scripture are, among others, the following:[63] the Assumption of the Blessed Virgin Mary;[64] validity of Baptism of heretics;[65] offering of a chalice of wine mixed with water as a usage followed by our Lord;[66] infant Baptism;[67] devotion to images;[68] those things essential to some

---

[59]This is the rationale behind the decree on the canonical Scriptures in the fourth session of the Council of Trent. See also Congar, *Tradition and Traditions*, p. 99.

[60]Cf. John 21:25.

[61]See Congar, *Tradition and Traditions*, p. 117 in reference to Bellarmine, among others; see also Gannon, *The Rule of Faith*, p. 7.

[62]See *Tradition and Traditions*, pp. 50-64.

[63]Obviously, this list is not exhaustive as to the doctrines, morals and customs which various authors historically have given.

[64]Pope Pius XII, *Munificentissimus Deus*. The doctrine of the Assumption poses particular difficulties for Congar which is manifest in his "wary" treatment of it, e.g. see *Tradition and Traditions*, p. 62, footnote 1.

[65]St. Cyprian, *Epistle*, 75 (ANF V, p. 397-402) and St. Augustine, *De Baptismo, contra Donatistas*, l. II, c. 12 (NPNF, IV, p. 430).

[66]St. Cyprian, *Epistle*, 62 (ANF V, p. 360ff) and the Council of Trent, Sess. XXII, c. 7 (Denz. 1748/945).

[67]St. Augustine, *De Peccatorum Meritis et Remissione, et de Baptismo Parvulorum*, passim (NPNF 5, beginning on p. 12); *De Gestis Pelagii*, XI (NPNF c. 23, 5:193); *De Gratia Christi, ed de Peccato Originali, contra Pelagium*, bk. II, cc. 3f and 19 ((NPNF 5:238 and 243) and Council of Trent, para. 4 (Denz. 1541/791). While there is no Scriptural teaching on infant Baptism, there are some passages which are used to

of the sacraments,[69] such as Confirmation,[70] Holy Orders and Extreme Unction;[71] the Virginity of Mary *post partum;*[72] the consecration of virgins;[73] prohibition of marriage after a vow of virginity;[74] the reception of Holy Communion from priests by the laity while the priests communicate themselves[75] and offering Holy Mass not only for the living but for the dead.[76] Given the absence of these doctrines, Scripture cannot be THE rule of faith since it lacks teachings which are necessary for salvation.[77]

---

indicate infant Baptism indirectly. Ludwig Ott in *Fundamentals of Catholic Dogma* lists I Cor. 1:16; Acts 16:15 and 33 and Acts 18:8.

[68] Among others, see Second Council of Nicaea (Denz. 600/302).

[69] ST III, q. 64, a. 2, ad 1.

[70] Even the institution of Confirmation as a sacrament is missing in Scripture.

[71] IV Sent., d. 7, q. 1, a. 3.

[72] Robert Bellarmine, *De Controversiis*, IV, 9.

[73] Lodovico Nogarola as noted by Congar in *Tradition and Traditions*, pp. 59.

[74] St. Epiphanius as noted by Congar in *Tradition and Traditions*, pp. 52. This would also be prohibited by the Natural Law since it would be contrary to justice.

[75] Council of Trent, sess. XIII, c. 8 (Denz. 1648/881).

[76] Council of Trent, sess. XXII, c. 2 (Denz. 1743/940). There are others listed by Congar (*Tradition and Traditions*, pp. 50-64). The rationalism and historicism of Congar (*Tradition and Traditions*, p. 61-64) unfortunately affects his judgment of the understanding of tradition (especially oral tradition) in prior historical periods and limits his ability to recognize the value of these doctrines not found in Scripture, particularly those considered to be of oral tradition. For instance he notes: "The idea of an exclusively oral tradition, by personal contact, of revealed truths never written down is a figment of the imagination" (Congar, *Tradition and Traditions*, p. 167 and also in that vein, see ibid, p. 63f).

[77] It is for this reason that the thesis of Congar and other authors that everything necessary for salvation is in some way in Scripture is untenable. Cf. Congar, *Meaning of Tradition*, p. 106.

F. Tradition as the Rule of Faith

Billot asserts that "tradition is the rule of faith."[78] This would appear to fit what is known as the "Vincentian Canon." St. Vincent of Lerins in his work, *Commonitorium*, written in 437 A.D., provides the following principle in order to constitute the rule of faith:

> In the Catholic Church itself, great care must be taken, that we hold that which has been believed everywhere, always, and by all. For this is truly and properly Catholic, which, as the force and notion of the name declares, almost all universally comprehend. But this at last becomes consent, if we follow the universal antiquity. Moreover, we follow universality in this way: if we confess that one true faith, which the whole Church throughout the world confesses; such is it with antiquity, if from those senses we in no way depart from what is manifest by our holy ancestors and fathers celebrated; so also it is the same with consent, if we adhere to the definitions and beliefs of all or almost all priests and doctors in that same antiquity.[79]

St. Vincent essentially establishes that the principle of judgment about what we are to believe is that which we have received from "our holy ancestors and fathers." In effect, it is tradition, i.e. that which has been handed on to us, which constitutes what we are to believe. For there is no aspect of what we believe as Catholics that was not passed on to us from those who went before us.

> For that holy and prudent man knew that to admit the notion of piety is nothing other than that everything is received by faith from the fathers and consigned by the same faith to the sons and [piety is] not our religion, which we want, that leads but more that which leads

---

[78] Billot, *De Immutabilitate Traditionis*, p. 28 (actually passim, but it is explicitly asserted here). Billot's position is in fact more refined than this, as we shall see below.

[79] St. Vincent of Lerins, *Commonitorium*, para. II: in ipsa item Catholica Ecclesia magnopere curandum est ut id teneamus quod ubique, quod semper, quod ab omnibus creditum est. Hoc est etenim vere proprieque catholicum, quod ipsa vis nominis ratioque declarat, quae omnia fere universiter comprehendit. Sed hoc ita demum fiet, si sequamur universitatem antiquitatem, consensionem. Sequemur autem universitatem hoc modo, si hanc unam fidem veram esse fateamur quam tota per orbem terrarum confitetur ecclesia; antiquitatem vero ita, si ab his sensibus nullatenus recedamus quos sanctos majoros ac patres nostros celebrasse manifestum est: consensionem quoque itidem, si, in ipsa vetustate, omnium vel certe pene omnium sacerdotum pariter et magistrorum definitiones sententiasque sectemur.

must be followed, for it is proper to Christian modesty and gravity not to pass on his own beliefs to those who come after him, but to preserve what has been received from his ancestors. What then was the issue of the whole matter? What but the usual and customary one? Antiquity was retained, novelty was rejected.[80]

Tradition, therefore, would be the rule.

G. The Magisterium
1. The Magisterium as THE Rule of Faith

Yet, modern authors are quick to point out that even when discussing the notion that tradition is the rule, tradition involves the official organ of tradition which is the Magisterium. Therefore, tradition by its very nature implies a Magisterium.[81] Some of the strongest statements in support of the proposition that the Magisterium is the rule of faith come from the Magisterium itself. The Holy Office has observed that "[the Church] has always given and proposed its dogmatic definitions as the certain and immutable rule of faith."[82] This line is very important to sort out. First, by "Church,"[83] they are merely referring to the Magisterium.[84] Second, it is not

---

[80]St. Vincent of Lerins, *Commonitorium*, para. VI: Intelligebat etenim vir sanctus et prudens, nihil aliud rationem pietatis admittere, nisi ut omnia, qua fide a patribus suscepta forent, eadem fide filiis consignarentur, nosque religionem non, qua vellemus, ducere, set potius, qua illa duceret, sequi oportere, idque esse proprium christianae modestiae et gravitatis, non sua posteris tradere sed a maioribus accepta servare. Quis ergo tunc universi negotii exitus? Quis utique, nisi usitatus et solitus? Retenta est scilicet antiquitas, explosa novitas.

[81]This observation will be key to sorting out the actual rule of faith *quoad nos* (i.e. with respect to us).

[82]*Collectanea S. Congregationis de Propaganda Fidei seu Decreta Instructiones Rescripta pro Apostolicis Missionibus*, v. I, p. 703, n. 1276 (1865): "suas enim dogmaticas definitiones edidit semper ac proposuit tamquam certam et immutabilem fidei regulam."

[83]The word "Church" is found immediately before the passage quoted.

[84]OCE, v. 5, p. 768: "The Catholic Doctrine Touching the Church as the Rule of Faith. The term Church, in this connection, can only denote the teaching Church, as is clear from the passages already quoted from the New Testament and the Fathers. But the teaching Church may be regarded either as the whole body of the episcopate, whether scattered throughout the world or collected in an ecumenical council, or it may be synonymous with the successor of St. Peter, the Vicar of Christ." In this respect, we may also say the Church is the rule of faith.

the Magisterium as such that is the rule, but the *definitions* of the Magisterium that are the rule. This avoids a certain intellectual confusion insofar as the office itself is not the rule but what the office teaches is the rule. If this is kept in mind, nothing prohibits one from referring to the Magisterium as the rule as long as one understands by that what the Magisterium teaches.[85]

St. Thomas observes that it pertains to the pope to say what is of the faith and to determine new editions of the symbols (Creed).[86] He also notes that the synods (councils) bind because the pope calls and confirms the propositions.[87] Clearly, if the pope does not sign or confirm the decrees of a council, they are not infallible. He also observes that the pope can say which propositions of others, (such as St. Athanasius, the Patristics or the Theologians), are of the faith. But he calls these propositions the *quasi* rule of faith because they rest upon the authority of the pope or Magisterium.[88] This is echoed in Pope Pius IX's *Tuas Libenter,*[89] where he says that we are to hold those teachings as pertaining to the faith, not only the decrees of the councils but the universal and constant consensus of the Catholic Theologians.

2. The *Current* Magisterium as Rule of Faith

Billot observes that the proximate and immediate rule of faith is the infallible and ever *living* Magisterium of the Catholic Church.[90] The notion of the living Magisterium asserts that the Magisterium will always be present in the Church, passing on the tradition. It is "living" because in each generation there are living members of the Magisterium who teach and preach the Deposit of Faith. Therefore, each generation is bound to the current or living

---

[85] It is a common way of speaking to refer to the Magisterium as the rule when what is understood is the teaching or definitions of the Magisterium. For instance we see this way of speaking exhibited by Pope Pius XII, in *Humanae Generis,* para. 18: "...this sacred Office of Teacher in matters of faith and morals must be the proximate and universal criterion of truth for all theologians, since to it has been entrusted by Christ Our Lord the whole deposit of faith—Sacred Scripture and divine Tradition—to be preserved, guarded and interpreted..."

[86] ST II-II, q. 1, a. 10. Cf. ST II-II, q. 5, a. 3.

[87] Ibid., ad 2.

[88] Ibid, ad 3.

[89] Denz. 2879/1683. See also Gregory IX, *Ab Aegyptiis* (Denz. 824/442); Sixtus IV, *Romani Pontificis provida* (Denz. 1407).

[90] Billot, *De Immutabilitate Traditionis,* p. 33. See also Congar, *Tradition and Traditions,* pp. 28, 205 and 303.

Magisterium. Sometimes this is called the *Magisterium quotidianum* insofar as it is the Magisterium that is alive today.

3. The *Prior* Magisterium as Rule

Yet, we may also say that the definitions of the prior Magisterium are a rule. By this we do not mean to divide the Magisterium into two parts, but to indicate that the members of the Magisterium in a certain period of history passed judgment on a particular article of faith. That judgment or definition then passes into the tradition and becomes as if a proper accident of the tradition. While it is not the Deposit itself, it does constitute the proper understanding of that particular aspect of the Deposit and therefore binds later generations as a rule regarding that particular teaching.[91]

4. The Magisterium is not THE Rule

From the aforesaid regarding God being THE rule, we see that the Magisterium, whether current or prior, is not THE rule of faith since it is a secondary rule in relation to God, Who is the primary rule. Congar is correct when he says "The Rule of Faith is the truth given and transmitted, which the pastors only guard, without their Magisterium itself being either considered or qualified as a 'rule of faith.'"[92] Here Congar does not mean to assert that in no way is the Magisterium a rule of faith, since elsewhere he asserts that it is.[93] What he is indicating is that it is the teaching which is passed on to which we must conform, not the Magisterium except insofar as it defines and teaches that doctrine. In this sense, the Magisterium is a rule since we must conform to its teaching which is none other than the teaching of God about Himself, i.e. revelation.

H. The *Sensus Fidelium* as the Rule of Faith

The *Catechism of the Catholic Church* states that

> The whole of the faithful cannot err (*falli*) and the whole people manifest this particular property mediating the supernatural *sensus fidei* when "from the bishops to the last of the lay faithful" it exhibits

---

[91]This will become more important as we discuss how the living or current Magisterium is bound to the tradition; see below.

[92]Congar, *Tradition and Traditions*, p. 28.

[93]Congar, *Tradition and Traditions*, pp. 148, 205 and 303. We are presuming that these passages from Congar are not meant to contradict each other but that Congar meant them to be mutually qualifying. See also Congar, *The Meaning of Tradition*, p. 68-71.

its universal consent of things pertaining to faith and morals.[94]

When the whole of the faithful consent to a particular doctrine, it is to be considered as pertaining to the faith. In this respect, it would be a rule of faith in relation to the specific doctrine in question.[95]

III. The Solution as to THE Rule of Faith

Given all of the different historical usages of the term "rule of faith," one must begin to ask the question what is, in fact, THE rule of faith? To beginning sorting this out, we may say that St. Thomas is correct that ultimately God is THE rule of faith, since He is the primary rule in relation to all secondary rules. When the Apostles received the Deposit of Faith, either from Christ (God) Himself[96] or by divine inspiration when writing the books of the New Testament, *for them*, THE rule of faith would be God Who reveals. But this Deposit was given to the Apostles in an act of tradition and does not come to us from God directly or proximately, but only remotely. Therefore, we must find the proximate rule of faith *quoad nos post Apostolos* (with respect to us after the Apostles) in order to ensure that our faith adheres to the rule.

A. Initial Distinctions

To begin sorting out the rule of faith, we can look at two distinctions that have been proposed in this area of discussion. The first is a distinction made between what is known as the *object* of faith and the *rule* of faith. Cardinal Billot makes this distinction by observing that the object is the truth to be believed and the rule formally considered is that which contains the truth to be believed and to which we must conform in believing. Hence, the object to be believed is the truth passed on by tradition and the rule is the tradition which contains and passes on that object. This tradition occurs in

---

[94]CCC, n. 92 (quoting Vatican II, *Lumen Gentium*, para. 12): " Universitas fidelium [...] in credendo falli nequit, atque hanc suam peculiarem proprietatem mediante supernaturali sensu fidei totius populi manifestat, cum 'ab Episcopis usque ad extremos laicos fideles' universalem suum consensum de rebus fidei et morum exhibet."

[95]Popes in the past have made use of the *sensus fidelium* in support of certain doctrines, e.g. see Pope Blessed Pius IX, *Ineffabilis Deus* (1854) and Pope Pius XII, *Munificentissimus Deus* (1950).

[96]This would also apply to some of the disciples who heard Christ's preaching, although they were not the official organ of transmission of the Deposit; the Apostles were.

the preaching of the Church or, more specifically,[97] the Magisterium, which is the official organ of tradition.[98] By "the object of faith," Cardinal Billot means that which is contained in tradition and Scripture[99] or, we may say broadly, tradition in the broadest sense, as including all of those things which are passed on in any way, which would include Scripture and tradition in the more restrictive sense.

The second distinction which is of importance is that which was somewhat common among the manualists and is often attributed to Franzelin, who gives an exemplary expression of it. Franzelin distinguishes between what he calls active tradition and the object of tradition.[100] This distinction does not differ essentially from Billot's distinction. But Franzelin goes on to distinguish between what he calls the proximate and remote rule of faith: "Scripture and Tradition (objective, comprehended in the monuments and documents) is the *remote rule of faith*; the Church (the living Magisterium of the Church and [its] preaching) is the *proximate rule of faith*."[101]

This passage contains several points of importance. The first is that Scripture and tradition are the remote rule but by this he means to include the monuments and documents. This indicates that by tradition he means to include all of the other aspects of tradition which are not essential to the Deposit of Faith but are passed on with it, such as the teachings of the Patristics, Theologians, judgments of the Magisterium as well as all of those things contained under the notion of monuments and documents.[102] If one takes the Tradition as indicated by Franzelin in this passage and Scripture together, then one is left with the prior distinction of tradition in the broad sense of all of those things passed on in some way.

B. THE Rule of Faith *Quoad Nos post Apostolos*

If we take Franzelin and Billot's distinctions and formulate them

---

[97]Billot, *De Immutabilitate Traditionis*, p. 22f.

[98]Ibid., p. 33.

[99]Ibid., p. 23, footnote 1.

[100]Franzelin, *Tractatus de Divina Traditione et Scriptura*, Thes. I, p. 12.

[101]Ibid., Thes. XIII, p. 155: "Scriptura et Traditio (Obiectiva, comprehensa in monumentis et documentis) est *regula fidei remota*; Ecclesia (vivens Ecclesiae magisterium et praedicatio) est *regula fidei proxima*." See also Congar, *Tradition and Traditions*, p. 199.

[102]Billot (*De Immutabilitate Traditionis*, p. 24) observes that the monuments are the remote rule.

together, we see that they actually express what is considered by some authors as THE rule of faith, formulated by Vatican I:

> Further divine and Catholic faith is all of those things to be believed which are contained in the written word of God or tradition and proposed by the Church either by the solemn judgment or by the ordinary universal magisterium, as divinely revealed to be believed.[103]

The position that this is THE rule of faith *quoad nos post Apostolos* is echoed by a variety of different authors.[104]

Considering all that we have said up to now, we are left with the conclusion that all of the rules of faith aforementioned come together in a single, coherent rule of faith. Since God reveals Himself and this is the primary rule, the primary rule is expressed and passed on by the secondary rule, which is the active tradition, to use Franzelin's term. The active tradition

---

[103]Vatican I, *Dei Filius*, c. 3 (Denz. 3011/1792): "Porro fide divina et catholica ea omnia credenda sunt, quae in verbo Dei Scripto vel traditio continentur et ab Ecclesia sive Solemni iudicio sive ordinario et universi magisterio tamquam divinitus revelata credenda proponuntur."

[104]Among others see, Pope St. Pius X, *Lamentabili*, prop. 4 and 5 (Denz. 3404/2004 and 3405/2005); Billot, *De Immutabilitate Traditionis*, p. 33; Franzelin, *Tractatus de Divina Traditione et Scriptura*, Thes. XIII, p. 155; Hervé, *Manuale Theologiæ Dogmaticæ*, vol. I, p. 536; Gannon, *The Rule of Faith*, p. 8f (Gannon quotes the Council of Trent to the same effects Vatican I) and Congar, *Tradition and Traditions*, p. 333f. Congar's position that the Magisterium is not THE rule and his criticism of Billot for linking the tradition and the Magisterium as the rule of faith is unfounded. His argument is that "the Magisterium has not given expression to everything that is relevant to our belief" (ibid., p. 335). This is not exactly true. While it may or may not be the case that the Magisterium has formally defined or spoken on each and every doctrine (which seems unlikely today but shall be conceded on the basis that there may be a period in history at the beginning of the Church when this was the case), the fact is that the Magisterium has always said that we must adhere to all of the Deposit of Faith. Moreover, the Second Council of Nicaea issued the anathema (4) "If anyone rejects any written or unwritten ecclesiastical tradition of the Church, let him be anathema" ("Εἴ τις πᾶσαν παράδοσιν ἐκκλησιατικὴν ἔγγραφον ἢ ἄγραφον ἀθετεῖ, ἀνάθεμα ἔστω"). Given that we must adhere to the Deposit, and given that one cannot reject any ecclesiastical tradition (for the Council of Nicaea, this includes tradition in the broadest sense of the term), then the Magisterium has given expression to the fact that we must adhere to all that is to be believed. Moreover, the Magisterium is the guardian and official organ of transmission of tradition, even when tradition is taken in the broad sense. The fourth anathema of the Second Council of Nicaea also indicates that the tradition is also a negative rule of faith insofar as one's proposition or belief can never contradict (reject) the ecclesiastical tradition.

possesses a unity of two aspects. The first is what was called the proximate rule of faith which is the current living Magisterium. But the current and living Magisterium passes to us the object, the tradition taken in the broad sense, i.e. Scripture and tradition in the more restrictive sense. By in the tradition "in the more restrictive sense", we understand that this includes the definitions and teachings of the prior Magisterium, which would include the formulation of revelation in the symbols or creeds, as well as the Deposit of Faith, i.e. those things necessary for salvation. It would also include all of the other monuments which have the current Magisterium as their guard and as their promoter. The theological virtue of faith then would be seen as the rule insofar as the proper object of the virtue of faith is the active tradition, i.e. the teaching of the current Magisterium (proximate rule) with the tradition taken in the broad sense (the remote rule – Scripture and tradition including all of the monuments and documents). The theological virtue of faith, as a rule, only indicates that it is corrupted, increased or fulfilled when it deviates from or adheres to the external rule (i.e. external to the individual possessing the faith), which is the active tradition, in the sense understood by Franzelin. Lastly, the *sensus fidelium* is nothing other than the action of the Holy Spirit through the collective inclination of the theological virtue of faith as it resides in each of the individuals possessing the theological virtue. Since the theological virtue is one as to its species,[105] then all of the faithful would be inclined to adhere to revelation, i.e. the object of faith as proposed by the Magisterium.

IV. Deviation from the Rule of Faith

Yet, in order to understand the rule of faith better, we need to consider a very difficult question, viz. what happens when a particular member of the Magisterium, including the pope, is discordant or deviates from the remote rule. When Vatican I was formulating the doctrine on papal infallibility, it had to deal with several historical cases in which popes had taught things that were erroneous or heretical. Among other cases, Martin I, along with the third Council of Constantinople, condemned the monothelitism of Pope Honorius I.[106] Also, there is the example of the condemnation of Nicolaus I who held that aside from the Trinitarian formula one could simply baptize "in nomine Christi."[107] Sometimes popes disagree on particular issues such as was

---

[105]ST, II-II, q. 4, a. 6.

[106]Denz. 487f/251f, 496-498/253, 518/271 and 550. These cases which we are about to mention can be found in OCE under the entry *Infallibility*.

[107]Denz. 646/211.

the case with Caelestinus III and Innocent III who disagreed over issues pertaining to the Pauline privilege.[108]

The historical reality of papal error and heresy forces us to consider what is the rule of faith for someone living under members of the Magisterium that are teaching error or heresy. Since normally the rule of faith is the teachings of tradition and Scripture as taught by the Magisterium, what does one do when the members of the Magisterium lapse into heresy? Normally we say that one is orthodox as long as one does not dissent from the teachings of the Magisterium (proximate rule).[109] Yet, this begs the question, since historically there have been members of the Magisterium who have lapsed into heresy and error.

In his commentary on Peter Lombard's *Sentences*, St. Thomas observes that

> as man ought to obey an inferior power in only those things which are not repugnant to a superior power, so also man ought to conform himself to the primary rule according to his mode. Man ought to conform himself to the secondary rule in those things which are not discordant from the primary rule. That in which it is discordant is no longer a rule and because of this he ought not assent to a prelate preaching contrary to the faith since it is discordant with the primary rule.[110]

This is merely a more formal formulation of the Scriptural dictum "we ought to obey God rather than men."[111] But what is of importance is that the secondary rule only remains a rule as long as it is commensurate with the primary rule, which of course is God. Therefore, in the consideration of the rule of faith, the distinction between the proximate and the remote rule is of

---

[108]Denz. 768/405.

[109]Franzelin, *Tractatus de Divina Traditione et Scriptura*, Thes. XXIII, p. 263.

[110]III Sent., d. 25, q. 2, a. 1d, ad 3: "sicut homo debet obedire inferiori potestati in his tantum in quibus non repugnat potestas superior; ita etiam debet homo se primae regulae in omnibus commensurare secundum suum modum; secundae autem regulae debet se homo commensurare in his in quibus non discordat a prima regula: quia in his in quibus discordat, jam non est regula; et propter hoc praelato contra fidem praedicanti non est assentiendum, quia in hoc discordat a prima regula."

[111]Acts 5:29.

prime importance.[112] We do not have a direct contact with God who is the primary rule. Therefore, if the proximate rule lapses, logically we are forced to fall back upon the remote rule since (a) it contains the judgments and teachings of the prior Magisterium which are commensurate with the primary rule and (b) it contains the Deposit of Faith, i.e. the revealed knowledge which God passed onto the Apostles.

Yet, St. Thomas also says that human knowledge is not the rule of faith[113] and this denies two propositions. The first is the proposition of the modernists that the rule of faith is immanent, i.e. within ourselves and so we judge what we are to believe based upon our own personal experience. The second is that it does not allow us to stand in judgment of the Magisterium, as if we were to become the new proximate rule. On the other hand, St. Thomas goes on to say that ignorance of the primary rule does not suffice and so we are not allowed to simply follow a member of the Magisterium blindly or ignorantly.[114] We are bound to know those things necessary for salvation, which are contained in Scripture and tradition. Therefore, since tradition also contains the teaching and definitions of the Magisterium, we are able to rest upon the prior Magisterial judgments in matters which are necessary for salvation. In other words, if a Magisterial member teaches us something which is clearly contrary to the tradition of the Church (the remote rule), we are to ignore that particular teaching and pray for him. People tend to do this

---

[112]Billot asserts that revelation was not intended by Christ to be proposed apart from the infallible office (*munus*) of the Magisterium and so that the object and rule are to be considered inseparable (*De Immutabilitate Traditionis*, p. 33f). As a result, one would not be able to distinguish between the remote rule (tradition in the broad sense) and the proximate rule (the Magisterium). This is why for Billot tradition consists in the Magisterial act (rule) of passing on the Deposit of Faith (object) rather than tradition being the remote rule distinct from the Magisterium (proximate rule). As to those things which are infallibly defined and proposed and those things which are taught by and after the Apostles, we concede this point. However, it is because of the historical facts that we are compelled to accept the distinction between proximate and remote rule as made by Franzelin when discussing matters that are not *de fide*, i.e. when the Magisterium does not define or infallibly propose some doctrine *and* in which a member of the Magisterium has lapsed into error or heresy. Normally, the remote and proximate rules are not to be distinguished. If one does distinguish them, they are only distinct when considered on the ontological order, or in a case of an error of one of the members of the Magisterium, since his error distinguishes his belief from the faith (tradition) of the Church. This distinction is of prime importance for the faith and salvation of the members of the Church in a time of heresy among the members of the Magisterium.

[113]ST II-II, q. 2, a. 6, ad 3.

[114]III Sent., d. 25, q. 2, a. 1d, ad 3.

"instinctively", i.e. it is part of the *sensus fidelium* to reject a teaching that is manifestly contrary to the remote rule,[115] e.g. we have often heard a bishop say that the issue of women's ordination is still open to discussion, whereas Pope John Paul II manifested in *Ordinatio Sacerdotalis* that the teaching that women cannot be priests is irreformable by virtue of the ordinary infallible Magisterium.[116] When we hear bishops saying that it is still open to discussion, we must fall back on the remote rule, which is the teaching of Pope John Paul II and the entire tradition regarding the matter.

St. Thomas also indicates that the living Magisterium of the Church is bound to the Deposit of Faith and the prior Magisterial definitions and teachings which are considered of the faith (*de fide*).[117] Here we begin to see the limits of the Magisterium, i.e. that they are bound to the Deposit and are not free to found a new faith or sacraments, or teach something contrary to the faith. In fact, during the First Vatican Council, Archbishop Salas observed that the power of the pope is limited by the natural and divine laws, the precepts of Christ, the good of the Church, right reason and the rule of faith and morals.[118] Essentially, this means that the pope and Magisterium are bound to the remote rule and their offices are inextricably connected to, for the promotion of and for the protection of the remote rule of faith. We must agree with Congar that, for the Council of Trent, traditions (we may say the remote rule) "constitute a norm for the magisterium itself."[119] In the use of Thomistic and later scholastic and manualist language, Congar says that "it

---

[115]This is, in fact, the basic theme of St. Vincent's *Commonitorium*. He establishes criteria by which the remote rule (that which is taught everywhere, always and by all) can be properly discerned in order to accept what is authentically part of the tradition while at the same time give an objective basis by which one can reject novelty, i.e. what goes against the remote rule.

[116]The Congregation for the Doctrine of the Faith observed in a response (*Responsum ad dubium circa doctrinam in Epist. Ap. 'Ordinatio Sacerdotalis' traditam*, in *L'Osservatore Romano*, 22 November, 1995, N.47, Vatican City; with accompanying English translation), in relation to the document *Ordinatio Sacerdotalis*, that the exclusion of women from the priesthood pertains to the Deposit of Faith (*ad fidei depositum pertinens*). See also the article "*Ordinatio Sacerdotalis*: Infallible?" by Jack Healy in the December 1996 issue of *Homiletic and Pastoral Review*.

[117]IV Sent., d. 17, q. 3, a. 1e; ibid., q. 27, q. 3, a. 3, ad 2; ST III, q. 64, a. 2, ad 3; *De ver.* q. 14, a. 10, ad 11.

[118]Mansi LII, pp. 579-80 and as quoted in Congar, *Tradition and Traditions*, p. 225.

[119]Ibid., p. 181. See also ibid., pp. 222 and 226.

[Church or Magisterium] is *regula regulans et regulata*, whereas objective tradition is purely *regula regulans (fidem Ecclesiae)*."[120] Hence, even though the Magisterium is a rule, it is ruled or we may say regulated by the tradition.[121]

The historical case of John XXII provides a paradigm for this discussion:

> In the last years of John's pontificate there arose a dogmatic conflict about the Beatific Vision, which was brought on by himself, and which his enemies made use of to discredit him. Before his elevation to the Holy See, he had written a work on this question, in which he stated that the souls of the blessed departed do not see God until after the Last Judgment. After becoming pope, he advanced the same teaching in his sermons. In this he met with strong opposition, many theologians, who adhered to the usual opinion that the blessed departed did see God before the Resurrection of the Body and the Last Judgment, even calling his view heretical. A great commotion was aroused in the University of Paris when the General of the Minorites and a Dominican tried to disseminate there the pope's view. ...In December, 1333, the theologians at Paris, after a consultation on the question, decided in favour of the doctrine that the souls of the blessed departed saw God immediately after death or after their complete purification; at the same time they pointed out that the pope had given no decision on this question but only advanced his personal opinion, and now petitioned the pope to confirm their decision. John appointed a commission at Avignon to study the writings of the Fathers, and to discuss further the disputed question. In a consistory held on 3 January, 1334, the pope explicitly declared that he had never meant to teach contrary to Holy Scripture or the rule of faith and in fact had not intended to give any decision whatever. Before his death he withdrew his former opinion, and declared his belief that souls separated from their bodies enjoyed in heaven the Beatific Vision.[122]

This may be said to be paradigmatic for several reasons. The first is that the pope taught the error during a Magisterial act, i.e. preaching. Second, he was in error, though we would not say formally heretical, since he lacked the

---

[120]Ibid., p. 205.

[121]See Congar, *The Meaning of Tradition*, pp. 64, 70f, 81 and 100.

[122]OCE, vol. VIII, p. 433ff under the entry "John XXII."

obstinacy which is required for formal heresy.[123] Third, the pope appointed a commission to examine the tradition, i.e. the rule of faith. This indicates that the pope recognized that even he is bound to the tradition. Therefore, we know that if a Magisterial member lapses into error or heresy, we are to follow the remote rule, which is tradition in the broad sense of the term.[124]

---

[123] CIC/1983, Can. 751. Cf. CIC/1917, Can. 1325.

[124] The requirement to return to the remote rule when in question about a teaching is stated in St. Vincent of Lerins' *Commonitorium* (para. III): Quid si in ipsa vetustate, duorum aut trium hominum, vel certe civitatis unius aut etiam provinciae alicujus error depredendatur? Tunc omnino curabit ut paucorum temeritati vel inscitiae, si qua sunt, universiter antiquitus universalis Ecclesiae decreta praeponat. Quid si tale aliquid emergat ubi nihil hujusmodi reperiatur? Tunc operam dabit ut collatas inter se majorum consulat interrogetque sententias, eorum duntaxat qui diversis licet temporibus et locis, in unius tamen Ecclesiae Catholicae communione et fide permanentes, magistri probabiles existerunt; et quicquid non unus aut duo tamen, sed omnes pariter uno eodemque consensu aperte, frequenter, perseveranter tenuisse, scripsisse, docuisse cognoverit, id sibi quoque intelligat absque ulla dubitatione credendum. (What if in antiquity itself error is found in two or three men, or certainly in one city or even some province? Then he will take care altogether that he universally proposes the decrees of antiquity of the universal Church, if there are any, to the temerity and ignorance of a few. What, if some such thing arise, where there is nothing of the kind discovered? Then he will confer, consult and examine the beliefs of the ancestors, of those precisely who, though living in diverse times and places, yet remaining in the communion and faith of the one Catholic Church, arise the demonstrations of the teachers; and whatsoever he shall ascertain to have been held, written, taught, not by one or two only, but by all, equally, with one consent, openly, frequently, persistently, that he also may understand that it is to be believed without any doubt.)

Chapter 2: The Tradition as Precept:
Binding Force of Tradition in General

The juridical concept of the deposit requires that it is not the property of the guardian. In other words, it is not the person who receives it that has ownership of it, but of the consigner who is handing it over to him to keep it in a safe state. The Deposit of Faith has come from God and has been entrusted to those to whom a special assistance of the Holy Spirit is assured, i.e. to those who succeed the Apostles and their Magisterium and in their ministry. Christ is the consignor and therefore has transmitted the deposit whose content cannot be subject to alteration. St. Paul refers to the Apostles as the "custodians of the Mysteries of God."[125] Being a custodian entails two essential functions: (1) to pass on and make available what was given, as St. Paul says, "tradidi enim vobis, in primis quod et accepi".[126] In this respect, the Magisterium is not permitted to block the passing on of doctrines. The very nature of the Magisterium is to pass on or to be an instrument of tradition. Yet, (2) they are to pass on *what they have received*, not their own teachings or their own alterations of the teachings of Christ.

Historically, the tradition of the Church is viewed as something in complete opposition to the Hegelian dialectic which insists that change cannot help but creep in. Some labor under the idea that each successive generation receives the Deposit, modifies it and then passes that on. This is contrary to the very divine mandate or command. Sacred Tradition, unchanged and unmodified, is not only a fact of history, but it is a matter of divine law. The divine law to pass on the tradition was given to the Apostles when Christ said, "Go therefore and make disciples of all the nations, baptizing them in the name of the Father and the Son and the Holy Spirit, teaching them to observe all things whatsoever I commanded you. And behold I am with you always, even to the consummation of the world."[127] In effect, Christ is mandating that everybody is to be proselytized, prudence being observed, of course. The Apostles and their successors are the guardians, the faithful dispensers, not the inventors, of the doctrine of Christ, conserving the doctrinal integrity of the teachings of Christ. This does not mean that he cannot give a fuller explanation of a particular doctrine but that what he has received cannot be changed.

St. Vincent of Lerins states it this way:

---

[125] I Cor. 4: 1-2.

[126] I Cor. 15: 3: I have passed on to you, first what I also received.

[127] Matthew 28: 19f.

For that holy and prudent man knew that to admit the notion of piety is nothing other than that everything is received by faith from the fathers and consigned by the same faith to the sons and not our religion, which we want, that leads but more that which leads must be followed, for it is proper to Christian modesty and gravity not to pass on his own beliefs to those who come after him, but to serve that which is accepted by his ancestors. What then was the issue of the whole matter? What but the usual and customary one? Antiquity was retained, novelty was rejected.[128]

When St. Vincent says "must be followed", he uses the words "sequi oportet"; "oportet" means "it is right/proper/necessary" or even "ought". Clearly, in this passage, St. Vincent sees the remote rule as something morally binding if it is necessary to follow or if one ought to follow it. What we want or think is not the standard or principle of judgment of what is to be believed, but whatever antiquity, which is known through tradition, tells us.

St. Robert Bellarmine in his *De Controversiis* provides a fuller understanding of exactly how the tradition binds:

Ecclesiastical traditions are properly called certain ancient customs, started by either prelates, or the people, which gradually by the tacit consent of the people obtained force of law. And indeed traditions have the same force as divine precepts, either divine doctrines written in the Gospels, and similarly the apostolic traditions non-written have the same force as the written apostolic traditions, as the Council of Trent in the fourth session asserts. ... Moreover ecclesiastical traditions have that same force as decrees and written constitutions of the Church.[129]

---

[128]St. Vincent of Lerins, *Commonitorium*, Chpt. VI (para. 16): Intelligebat etenim vir sanctus et prudens, nihil aliud rationem pietatis admittere, nisi ut omnia, qua fide a patribus suscepta forent, eadem fide filiis consignarentur, nosque religionem non, qua vellemus, ducere, set potius, qua illa duceret, sequi oportere, idque esse proprium christianae modestiae et gravitatis, non sua posteris tradere sed a maioribus accepta servare. Quis ergo tunc universi negotii exitus? Quis utique, nisi usitatus et solitus? Retenta est scilicet antiquitas, explosa novitas.

[129]*De Controversiis*, Book IV, Chpt. 2: Ecclesiasticae Traditiones proprie dicuntur consuetudines quaedam antique, vel a Praelatis, vel populis inchoatae, quae paulatim tacito consensu populorum vim legis obtinuerunt. Et quidem Traditiones divinae eandem vim habent, quam divine praecepta, sive divina doctrina scripta in Evangeliis, et similiter apostolicae Traditiones non scriptae eamdem vim habent, quam apostolicae Traditiones scriptae, ut Concilio Trident. Sess. 4. asseritur. ...Ecclesiasticae

This passage is loaded and contains several things of importance. (1) The use of the word "force" or "vis" in Latin indicates that one is compelled or bound to do something. (2) In the context of the use of his word "precepts", what is indicated is that this binding force is in the forum of the conscience insofar as we are bound to accept what is passed on to us on the side of the tradition as a matter of precept or law. Essentially, refusal to accept what is passed on AS it is passed on constitutes a violation of the divine law, i.e. it is sinful. Moreover, (3) those who are entrusted, i.e. the custodians of the mysteries of Christ, are bound to pass on by precept what they have received. If a custodian, i.e. a member of the Magisterium, refuses to pass on what he has received, then he sins. If he modifies or alters it, he sins.

St. Robert also indicates that (4) there are different traditions and from this we are to understand that different traditions have a different degree of binding force based upon the source of the tradition and the nature of what is passed on. Different kinds of tradition and different objects of tradition bind in differing degrees and in different ways. Violation of the tradition does not apply equally to all aspects of the tradition, but all of it binds under the pain of sin, either venial or mortal. What is also important to recognize is that the binding in the forum of conscience pertains not just to the Deposit of Faith, but also what is has been accrued to the tradition by means of papal teachings, the theological work of saints, etc. In effect, what becomes binding to pass on under sin is the totality of the tradition.

This being said, we realize that the question of theological notes is key. A theological note is the name given by which the certitude of the particular doctrine is known or we may say that different doctrines have different degrees of certitude based upon author, Church pronouncements, etc. and the degree of the certitude of the doctrine is known as its theological note.

Ludwig Ott in his *Fundamentals of Catholic Dogma* gives a basic outline of the various doctrines and their theological notes[130]:

> The highest degree of certainty appertains to the immediately revealed truths. The belief due to them is based on the authority of God Revealing (*fides divina*), and if the Church, through its teaching, vouches for the fact that a truth is contained in Revelation, one's certainty is then also based on the authority of the Infallible Teaching Authority of the Church (*fides catholica*). If Truths are defined by a solemn judgment of faith (definition) of the Pope or of a General Council, they are *de fide definita*. Catholic truths or Church doctrines,

---

autem Traditiones eandem vim habent, quam decreta, et constitutiones Ecclesiae scripturae.

[130]P. 9f. Various quotes regarding these notes are taken from Ott.

on which the infallible Teaching Authority of the Church has finally decided, are to be accepted with a faith which is based on the sole authority of the Church (*fides ecclesiastica*). These truths are as infallibly certain as dogmas proper.

It is hard to see how denial of any of these *de fide definita* statements would not constitute grave matter in the forum of conscience, i.e. we are bound to give assent to them under pain of mortal sin. An example of a *de fide* proposition given by God would be the doctrine of the Eucharist in John 6.

Yet, there are also *de fide non-definita* statements which bind the person likewise under pain of mortal sin. Pius IX in *Tuas Libenter* states that not only the decrees of the councils and popes and ordinary Magisterium throughout the whole world but also that which is the (1) universal and (2) constant consensus of theologians is also to be held as pertaining to the faith.[131] It is important to note that something does not have to be *de fide definita* in order for assent to be required absolutely, i.e. some things in revelation come directly from the authority of God and may not be formally defined by the Church but that does not mean one is not bound to believe them, e.g. that Christ had the power to heal or command the elements as in walking on water and calming the storm.

A theological censure is a judgment "which characterizes a proposition touching Catholic Faith or Moral Teaching as contrary to Faith or at least as doubtful." Theological censures are of two kinds, viz. an authoritative or a judicial judgment and a private doctrinal judgment. An authoritative or judicial judgment is one on which the teaching authority i.e. the Magisterium within the Church, has made a pronouncement. A private doctrinal judgment is that which is pronounced by the theological science and by that is meant the various saints and theologians throughout history which have made statements about the truth or falsity of a particular proposition. A proposition in opposition to a *de fide* proposition is called a heretical proposition (*propositio haeretica*). This proposition is opposed to a formal dogma; and as such to give assent to such a proposition would be considered sinful, normally mortal. The gravity arises from the fact that it is contrary to the theological virtue of faith, corrupts it[132] and therefore blocks one's ability

---

[131]Denz. 2879/1683: universali et constanti consensus a catholicis theologis ad fidem pertinere retinentur.

[132]The term "corrupt" here is being used in the formal philosophical sense. The colloquial use of the term corrupt normally means to render bad or evil but here it does not mean that. "To corrupt" in the formal philosophical sense means to cause the thing to go out of existence. See Wuellner, *A Dictionary of Scholastic Philosophy*, p. 67.

to enter heaven since one cannot enter heaven without faith.[133] As was observed above, the full assent to a single heretical proposition corrupts one's faith.

After the *de fide* proposition is the teaching which is proximate to the faith (*sententia fidei proxima*) which is doctrine "which is regarded by theologians generally as a truth of Revelation, but which has not yet been finally promulgated as such by the Church." A proposition contrary to *sententia fidei proxima* propositions are called a "proposition proximate to heresy" (*propositio heresi proxima*). Because *sententia fidei proxima* propositions come from revelation, even though they are not defined, denial of them is grave matter based upon the principle of obedience to God (part of which is our moral obligation to submit our intellect to truths which He reveals) as well as the denial of them corrupts faith since faith is essentially ordered to giving assent to what is revealed.[134]

The next level of theological certainty of a doctrine is called a "teaching pertaining to the Faith, i.e., theologically certain (*sententia ad fidem pertinens, i.e., theologice certa*)". This is a proposition which the Magisterium has not defined but "whose truth is guaranteed by its intrinsic connection with the doctrine of revelation (theological conclusions)". To deny a *theologice certa* proposition is to deny a doctrine of revelation by way of conclusion. An example of a theologically certain doctrine is that , e.g. everyone has their own guardian angel.[135] A proposition which denies a *theologice certa* proposition is called a "proposition savouring of or suspect of heresy (*propositio haeresim sapiens or de haeresi suspecta*)". The reason it is suspect or savoring of heresy is because, if one draws the natural conclusion from the proposition, one will end up denying a proposition which the Magisterium has pronounced upon. Normally, these kinds of propositions constitute grave matter because of the connection to the Magisterial teaching.

The next level of theological certainty and therefore binding force of a teaching is called a "Common Teaching (*sententia communis*)". This is doctrine which in itself belongs to the field of free opinions, but which is accepted by theologians generally. As Ott observes:

> Theological opinions are free views on aspects of doctrines concerning Faith and morals, which are neither clearly attested in Revelation nor decided by the Teaching Authority of the Church.

---

[133]Without faith, you cannot be saved. See John 3:36.

[134]For a further discussion, see Ripperger, *Introduction to the Science of Mental Health*, vol. II, chpt. 4.

[135]Ott, op. cit, p. 120.

Their value depends upon the reasons adduced in their favor (association with the doctrine of Revelation, the attitude of the Church, etc.). A point of doctrine ceases to be an object of free judgment when the Teaching Authority of the Church takes an attitude which is clearly in favor of one opinion.[136]

Yet, there are differing levels of theological opinion. Some, such as *sententia communis*, cannot simply be dismissed without good reason, since to do so would be to fall into an "Erroneous Proposition" (*propositio erronea*). This is a proposition which is "opposed to a truth which is proposed by the Church as a truth intrinsically connected with a revealed truth (*error in fide ecclesiastica*), or opposed to the common teaching of theologians (*error theologicus*)". In order to deviate from the common teaching of theologians, there must be substantive reasons for doing so. If one deviates from the common teaching of theologians, his opinion is known as "a Temerarious Proposition (*propositio temeraria*), i.e., deviating without reason from the general teaching." This is one area which has constituted a real problem since the Second Vatican Council.

The degree of binding force on this aspect of the tradition becomes more difficult to ascertain. On one level, these and other propositions of lesser theological note fall within the domain of free opinion. However, that does not mean that propositions taught in the tradition can be dismissed out of hand or without a sufficient reason with impunity. Since the theologians that went before us, building upon the tradition of centuries regarding the discussion of specific topics, reasoned carefully to conclusions which become the common teaching, then to reject the common teaching without a sufficient reason falls prey to impiety, as will be discussed below. Moreover, as prudence requires docility, then normally, one should submit his intellect to the work of the Theologians and saints through out history. Given the aforesaid, ascribing the moral binding force of the tradition in regard to common teachings is based upon two things. The first is subjective, insofar as one's own moral dispositions (docility, piety, etc.) are in place when considering these propositions. However, the second, i.e. the objective content, of a moral obligation to accept the particular common teaching would vary greatly depending upon several factors, such as: (1) the number of Theologians and saints who held to such a position; (2) the particular Theologians or saints that held the position, for some Theologians and saints are generally regarded to have greater insight and grasp of the divine realities and an ability to explicate them than others; (3) the gravity of the teaching discussed, for those matters touching upon key doctrines and grave moral

---

[136] Ott, op. cit., p. 10.

38

issues would bind more greatly than those about doctrines not required for salvation or speculation about venial sins and imperfections; (4) the closeness the particular doctrine has to some Magisterial pronouncement, for some common opinions deal with matters closely connected to what has been defined, while others are more remote. There may be other considerations not delineated here which would determine the binding force of a particular common opinion. However, it is safe to say that certain deviations from the common teaching would be grave without a sufficient reason while others would be venial. Contempt arising from impiety and indocility arising out of pride, etc., could render grave even some matter which would normally bind only under pain of venial sin. However, lacking any negative subjective factors, the binding force would be assessed based upon the objective criteria.

The next set of degrees of certainty have less binding force but due attention should be given to them.

> Theological opinions of lesser grades of certainty are called probable, more probable, well-founded (*sententia probabilis, probabilior, bene fundata*). Those which are regarded as being in agreement with the consciousness of Faith of the Church are called pious opinions (*sententia pia*). The least degree of certainty is possessed by the tolerated opinion (*opinio tolerata*), which is only weakly founded, but which is tolerated by the Church.

Other than the last degree of certainty, the remaining degrees should normally be treated with some degree of respect insofar as they come from our fathers in faith, i.e. as a matter of piety. Here, the primary considerations are the subjective factors of the individual who considers them. Rejection of these would not be sinful, generally speaking, but could be if the person does so out of impiety or some other vice. One can refuse to accept an *opinio tolerata* and still be without sin. Those propositions which reject the *sententia pia* are called "Proposition[s] Offensive to pious ears (*propositio piarum aurium offensiva*), i.e., offensive to religious feeling". In the last 40 years or so, often theologians, priests, etc., have made statements which were offensive to pious ears, e.g. recently it was proposed that the flight into Egypt by the Holy Family constituted an act of illegal immigration.[137]

Ott goes on to make three more distinctions regarding propositions which are negative in judgment. The first is called "a Proposition badly expressed (*propositio male sonans*), i.e., subject to misunderstanding by reason of its method of expression". Many theologians have maintained that some of the statements made in the documents of the Second Vatican Council suffer

---

[137] Any cursory search on the internet will provide ample discussion of this proposition.

from this difficulty. Recent attempts to clarify them by appealing to the tradition, even on the part of the Holy Father with his "hermeneutic of continuity", indicate a recognition that certain statements need clarification.

The next distinction regarding negative propositions is what is called "a Captious Proposition (*propositio captiosa*), i.e., reprehensible because of its intentional ambiguity". Again, some theologians accuse certain doctrinal statements of the Second Vatican Council of this difficulty, e.g. in Lumen Gentium,[138] we read: "This Church constituted and organized in the world as a society, subsists in the Catholic Church..." The use of the word subsist has set off a large amount of discussion resulting in many claiming that it is a word that is ambiguous. Regardless of the word's history in ecclesiology, the actual meaning of the word is debated to such a degree that one could legitimately conclude that it is ambiguous.[139]

The last distinction regarding negative propositions is what is called "a Proposition exciting scandal (*propositio scandalosa*)". Many faithful have heard these kinds of statements from the pulpit in recent years. A common one is when priests or even bishops suggest that the teaching of tradition on contraception by Paul VI is still open to discussion.[140]

To return to the discussion of the binding force, Billot says that the tradition has the notion of an obligatory rule of faith.[141] Something is said to be obligatory because it comes from the Latin word *ligare* which means to bind and in this case it binds morally, i.e. in the forum of conscience. Failure to engage in active tradition on the side of the Magisterium as to that which they have received or to ensure its integrity and its passing, constitutes something sinful, either as a form of heresy, therefore contrary to the virtue of faith, or as a form of negligence. On the side of the passive tradition, we are

---

[138] Para. 8.

[139] See Congregation for the Doctrine of the Faith, Responses to Some Questions Regarding Certain Aspects of the Doctrine on the Church, 2007. This document seeks to clarify this very issue.

[140] Paul VI merely gave expression to what was the constant teaching of the Church through its entire history regarding contraception. Its constant historical presence in the teaching of the Church is a clear indication that the teaching that the use of contraception constitutes a mortal sin is *de fide non definita* at least. This is said with the recognition that there is a discussion by some that the *Humanae Vitae* teaching on contraception is *de fide definita*, e.g. see Fr. Brian Harrison, "Ex Cathedra Status of the Encyclical 'Humanae Vitae'" in *Faith and Reason*, vol. XIX, no. 1; Spring 1993.

[141] *De Immutabilitate Traditionis contra Modernam Haeresim Evolutionismi*, p. 30.

obligated because of necessity to have faith for salvation, to accept all those things necessary for salvation on the side of the tradition.

In the same vein, in one of the greatest tracts ever written on Sacred Tradition, Ioannis Franzelin makes the following observation:

> From the opposite, therefore, the obedience of faith corresponds to this authority in believers not as a free option but under the distinction of necessary for eternal salvation.[142]

Obedience of faith is something binding the person in such a manner that if he does not give assent to what he is required to give assent to, he places his eternal salvation in jeopardy.[143] This applies, even to the current members of the Magisterium, for they stand in relationship to the prior tradition as believers and therefore are bound under the obedience of faith to those traditions. They stand as an authority *to which* that tradition was passed on the side of passive tradition and so they are bound to give assent. This assent then determines their acts of active tradition in which they stand as authority *from which* the tradition proceeds. This obedience of faith binds in the forum of conscience and therefore binds under the pain of sin, even the members of the Magisterium in every generation.

Fr. Agius makes an observation that is quite important for our understanding and our disposition towards the tradition:

> All Traditions, which are approved by the Church, whether they are Divine or Divine-apostolic, simply-apostolic or Ecclesiastical, command our respect and veneration. It is true, only the Divine or Divine-apostolic traditions contain in themselves to the revealed word of God, and constitute the object of our faith; but, it is not less true that all simply-apostolic and ecclesiastical traditions are based on a supernatural power and authority. *This supernatural authority or power is in itself a revealed truth.* It must, therefore, be obeyed. "He

---

[142] Franzelin, *Tractatus de Divine Traditione et Scriptura*, p. 25: Huic igitur auctoritati ex adverso respondet obedientia fidei in credentibus non liberae optionis, sed sub discrimine aeternae salutis necessaria.

[143] It is not only necessary for salvation, but what the modern experiment is showing us is that it is also necessary for spiritual progress as well as for understanding the faith. Without dependence upon the knowledge gained by the saints about the mechanics of the spiritual life, most people simply do not have the intellectual wherewithal nor the grace to be able to know how to progress in the spiritual life without the aid of the knowledge passed on to us by the saints. It is also true of intellectual advance.

that heareth you, heareth Me, and he that despiseth you despiseth Me."[144]

There are two important points to take from this passage. The first is that the prior Magisterium must be obeyed since the authority with which it promulgated teachings and establish traditions was a supernatural authority. The second is that this authority and these traditions command, i.e. bind us in conscience, to respect and veneration.

Agius goes on to say:

a man who rejects a simply-apostolic or ecclesiastical tradition, for instance, the ceremonies in the administration of the sacraments, the signing of the cross, holy water or other traditions, already approved by the church, denies at the same time her revealed authority. He, therefore, violates the Faith.[145]

When it comes to all other aspects about the tradition, we are bound morally to give assent to what is proposed and the degree of binding force of that assent is proportionate to the theological note. Agius then observes that for this reason: "all traditions, then, approved by the Church, must be respected and believed."[146]

In the context of the hierarchy, the living Magisterium is, in fact, the official organ of tradition; but the members of current Magisterium are also bound to the remote rule of faith in the forum of conscience. Of those matters which pertain to mere ecclesiastical traditions, they are bound in the forum of conscience to adhere to them unless there is a sufficient reason to the contrary and these ecclesiastical traditions should not be changed lightly. St. Thomas Aquinas observes that the changing of the law too frequently erodes the force of the law.[147] But the same thing can also be said of the tradition, even the ecclesiastical traditions: by changing those matters which pertain to the Sacred Tradition, regardless of their degree of theological note or importance, without sufficient reason, will undermine the understanding and binding force of the tradition, not just in the minds of the laity or the clergy but in the minds of the members of the Magisterium itself.

Even the papal oath reflected this understanding:

---

[144] Agius, *Tradition and the Church*, p. 12.

[145] Ibid., p. 12.

[146] Ibid., p. 13.

[147] ST I-II, q. 97.

I vow to change nothing of the received Tradition, and nothing thereof I have found before me guarded by my God-pleasing predecessors, to encroach upon, to alter, or to permit any innovation therein;

To the contrary: with glowing affection as her truly faithful student and successor, to safeguard reverently the passed-on good, with my whole strength and utmost effort;

To cleanse all that is in contradiction to the canonical order that may surface;

To guard the Holy Canons and Decrees of our Popes as if they were the Divine ordinances of Heaven, because I am conscious of Thee, Whose place I take through the grace of God, Whose Vicarship I possess with Thy support, being subject to the severest accounting before Thy Divine Tribunal over all that I shall confess;

I swear to God Almighty and the Saviour Jesus Christ that I will keep whatever has been revealed through Christ and His Successors and whatever the first councils and my predecessors have defined and declared.

I will keep without sacrifice to itself the discipline and the rite of the Church. I will put outside the Church whoever dares to go against this oath, may it be somebody else or I.

If I should undertake to act in anything of contrary sense, or should permit that it will be executed, Thou willst not be merciful to me on the dreadful Day of Divine Justice.

Accordingly, without exclusion, We subject to severest excommunication anyone – be it ourselves or be it another – who would dare to undertake anything new in contradiction to this constituted evangelic Tradition and the purity of the Orthodox Faith and the Christian Religion, or would seek to change anything by his opposing efforts, or would agree with those who undertake such a blasphemous venture.[148]

This text is a clear indication of how the Church understood the tradition even in connection to the members of the Magisterium. The Church use to require the pope to take the oath that he would give assent, both intellectually and morally, to the tradition in all respects as well as to venerate with "glowing affection" the tradition. In fact, the authority of the Magisterium by its very nature is ordered toward binding what it passes on, but it is also bound by what is passed to it.

---

[148] As quoted in Ferrara and Woods, *The Great Facade: Vatican II and the Regime of Novelty in the Roman Catholic Church*, p. 161-162.

When we stand back and consider this, we can say that as individuals, we not only have an obligation to give assent to and have respect for all aspects of the tradition intellectually, but that giving of assent to and having respect for are volitional acts and therefore bind morally. Conversely, we may say it is a manifestation of a moral problem if a particular individual will simply not adhere to the tradition (i.e. any aspect of the tradition) out of some type of obstinacy or unwillingness to do so. Spiritually this means that we must be willing to die to ourselves if we are truly going to adhere to the tradition.

But in a period in which new theories and new teachings abound all the more, we must ask ourselves how must we approach these new theories in relationship to the tradition. We may say that given what has been stated above there is a general principle which not only has intellectual but also moral binding force, which is: when a new theory is *praeter traditionem* (aside from the tradition) or *contra traditionem* (contrary to the tradition), favor or benefit of the doubt is always on the side of the tradition. This indicates that the benefit of the doubt or favor in giving assent is not on the side of the new theory due to the very nature and danger of novelty. Again, unless there is a sufficient reason, we are bound to hold even those of lower theological notes.

Chapter 3: Sins against the Tradition:
Binding Force of Tradition *in Species*

If the tradition has moral binding force, we must ask ourselves what specific sins and even which Commandments one sins against if one rejects, does not follow or does not venerate the tradition. First let us observe that both active and passive tradition sets up a set of virtues in the individual that willingly engages in the tradition. In other words, in passive tradition when one receives the tradition regularly, a set of habits is established in the children, among the faithful and even among ecclesiastics, resulting in a recognition that tradition is a good thing and it becomes a thing of joy, regardless if part of what is received is a discipline that requires self-denial. Our current generation, however, is in the habit of novelty and that is why tradition is so difficult for many of them, because the tradition is not just a thing, but an action, i.e. it is a way of living. Novelty ultimately militates against virtue because it does not seek good habits but intellectual or appetitive delight in the new thing. Insofar as novelty is against virtue, it is against the natural law and violates the different Commandments pertaining to the Decalogue. But the same thing can also be said of the active tradition, insofar as those who regularly engage in the active tradition according to the precepts of our Lord and of the Church have developed many virtues, as will be seen. Whereas those to whom the active tradition is entrusted but who do not pass on intact what was entrusted to them can easily succumb to vice.

A. Sins Against Faith

When a person does not accept the Sacred Tradition which is passed to him or does not pass on what has been entrusted to him, he sins against the virtue of faith. For faith is the supernatural virtue infused in the intellect by which we give assent to what is revealed. Yet, what is revealed is passed on by means of the tradition and therefore the virtue of faith requires that we give assent to what pertains to Sacred Tradition. But at certain times in history and particularly in modern times, there has been a rejection of the tradition, an introduction of novelty and constant changing of everything from doctrinal formulations to the monuments. Because the monumental structure of churches has changed, often what people believe has changed. Since monuments manifest our faith (like the liturgy), if the monuments are modified too much, one can be left with the impression that the faith has changed. The monuments themselves are a form of expression of faith and embody the faith in a visible matter. When these visible manifestations of the faith are attacked or changed, psychologically people feel their faith attack or changed. Therefore, if a person rejects any part of the tradition by refusing to accept everything, from the monuments to the doctrinal formulations, he sins against faith, not only insofar as these attacks are very often an expression against the faith or even a manifestation of one's own lack of faith, it is an attack on the faith of those who built the monument or those who formulated the doctrine and it is also an attack on the faith of those who should receive those monuments or formulations of doctrine to give greater clarity, stability and certainty to their faith.

B. Sins against Hope

There are many ways in which rejection of the tradition is a sin against hope, but we will only focus on two aspects of it here. The first has to do with the stability of the monuments and formulations of doctrine. If the tradition remains intact and the monuments are passed on intact as well as the doctrinal formulations without variation except to provide greater clarity, it provides a certainty on the side of the hearer that the faith does not change. As one views the generations upon generations which held the same faith, died holy deaths and sacrificed to provide for subsequent generations, great hope is engendered in the believer. But when the sands of teaching are constantly shifting and when the monuments are destroyed or attacked, the stability of the faith is lost and hope will decline.

Hope is the supernatural virtue infused in the will by which we await the promises of God and the aid which He will supply.[149] When one sees the consistency of the faith as engendered in the monuments and in the doctrinal formulations without variation, it is a rock upon which one can found one's pursuit of salvation. But if things change, or if, even worse, the tradition is rejected and people are told that those matters pertaining to the tradition are bad, the person's interior intellectual stability in relationship to the faith is undermined. The person begins to wonder if God really will provide what all the generations said He would when the various means of salvation seem to be removed. For example, when the devotions which were often the hallmark of prior generations were suddenly stopped or even characterized as bad, the hope, which people had through those devotions which often included promises from our Lord or Lady, very often collapsed. In this sense, rejection of the tradition can lead to despair, because the means of salvation are in the tradition and will not be found anywhere else. Therefore, if the tradition is rejected, the means of salvation are rejected and therefore hope will be lost.

We can see tremendous presumption on the side of those who change the tradition contrary to divine precept. Presumption results in one believing in one's own ability, without divine aid, to reach eternal beatitude.[150]

---

[149] For an expanded treatment of the issue, see Ripperger, *Introduction to the Science of Mental Health*, vol. II, chpt. 4, p. 368.

[150] ST II-II, q. 21, a. 1.

Presumption is caused directly by pride,[151] which is the overestimation of one's good or excellence. One thinks himself more than merely human or he overestimates the good or excellence of human nature. Since the tradition is provided by God as an external (or what is sometimes called an objective) grace, to reject the tradition or to act as if it is not necessary to give assent to it is to place oneself in a position where one can presume that he can survive spiritually, morally or even save his soul without the tradition. There is great presumption among those who destroy the monuments as if it was their place to destroy the product of generations of faith and piety. To act contrary to the tradition, to overhaul it and constantly change it, even in small matters as if it is at one's own discretion, is presumption. To do so manifests a complete lack of understanding what God's full intent and will is regarding these matters. Assaulting the tradition as well as making wide scale liturgical changes is analogous to opening the hood of a car and looking inside. One sees a number of wires, hoses, and various other indiscernible things. Lacking any clue about what they are there for and how they function, the person decides that he does not like it because it does not submit to his understanding, his view of order or his appetitive likes. So he starts pulling the wires out and then wonders why the car does not run as it should. This is what has happened in the last two generations. This is why one is never to presume that he knows what he is doing. There is a general moral principle: when in doubt of fact, do not act. If one does not know why a particular thing is there, one does not touch it. Those who pass on the tradition have an obligation to be selfless in relation to the tradition. What needs to be realized is that the tradition is not about us; it is about God and the salvation of our souls.

C. Sins against Charity

One of the primary reasons for the charism of infallibility is to make sure that the faith is passed on intact from generation to generation. The use of infallibility is to protect the faith and to ensure its orthodoxy so that those who give assent to those teachings which are infallibly defined may be assured that they believe rightly and will be saved. To provide that protection is a matter of charity.

Charity is defined as the supernatural virtue infused in the will by which the person loves God and one's neighbor for the sake of God. If one loves God and loves one's neighbor, one will always make sure the tradition is passed on intact for the greatest assurance possible of the salvation of those who receive that tradition. Even the very construction of monuments was often done for the love of God and therefore to destroy a monument without a sufficient reason is a sin against charity, i.e. a sin against the love of God. But

---

[151]ST II-II, q. 21, a. 4.

it is also a sin against one's neighbor who is deprived of the magnificent monument which would inspire him and lift his mind and heart to pray and to love God.

If one loves one's neighbor, he will want to ensure that his neighbor receives the tradition as fully as possible for the sake of his salvation. The extensive recent changes in the tradition have rendered the saving of our souls more difficult, which is against charity. The assault on the monuments as well as the doctrinal clarity on faith and morals taught by the Church has ravaged the affections which people have for the things of the faith and to which they have been attached in a rightly ordered manner. The impact it has had on people is clearly against charity and cannot be interpreted in any other way than sinful, often gravely sinful, especially when we are talking about the contempt with which these things were changed as well as the contempt shown to those who were attached to them in a rightly ordered manner.

D. Sins against Prudence

Prudence is defined as the virtue by which one knows the means to attain the end and prudence is made up of several integral parts.[152] There are different ways in which one sins against prudence in relationship to these integral parts. One of the integral parts of prudence is what is called the virtue of memory. The virtue of memory is the virtue by which one remembers the right things at the right time in order to act prudently. But the rejection of the tradition militates against the virtue of memory itself. In fact, one can say that tradition is the perpetuation of the memory of generations.

Another integral part of prudence is docility, which is defined as the virtue by which one is willing to be led. Modernism which is rooted in self refuses to submit to another which is the root cause of the sin against the tradition of not receiving it intact and unaltered from the remote rule, i.e. the prior Magisterium. Modernism, with its principle of immanence, has caused people to be focused on themselves, their own feelings and their own thoughts. It is not possible to accept the tradition based upon the principle of immanence for several reasons. One of these is that when one is focused on oneself, one is not focused on what is external to oneself. But the tradition is precisely something received from the outside. As people develop habits based upon the principle of immanence, they cannot be led because that is something from the outside. In effect, modernism with its principle of immanence renders people ungovernable and unteachable. Without a doubt, on a psychological level, modernism is one of the most effective weapons against the tradition.

---

[152] For discussion of the nature of prudence and its integral parts, see Ripperger, *Introduction to the Science of Mental Health*, vol. III, part II, chpt. 1.

Another virtue under prudence is called foresight, which is the virtue by which one is able to foresee the effects of a particular kind of action. Tradition and history tell us what happens when one deviates from the tradition itself; in other words, history and tradition tell us that, if one deviates from the tradition, bad things happen. When wholesale changes were made in the liturgy and in the life and discipline of the Church, those responsible lacked foresight which would have looked at past experience to know what evils could arise. This led to sins of incaution, which occur when people do not apply knowledge to action in order to avoid impediments and evils. Clearly, when one considers the extent of the changes made since the Second Vatican Council, one is struck with what appears to be a certain recklessness or even audacity.

The changes also lacked circumspection, which is the virtue by which one keeps track of his circumstances. One of the circumstances is place and in relationship to place, we stand in the position of an inferior in relationship to the prior Magisterium and to the tradition in our obligation to receive what is passed to us. But many do not know their place in the sense that they think they stand in a relationship of superiority to those who went before them. It is a sign of pride that many members of the Church think that they are superior to those who went before them and therefore stand in a position to pass judgment on what was handed to them by prior generations.

There has been a violation of the virtue of supernatural prudence by the obscurity of teaching in documents coming out of the Magisterium, which is a reflection of carnal prudence. There exists this idea that if they do not tone down doctrinal expressions, modify the rite of the Mass to accommodate modern man, stop evangelizing the Jews or the Orthodox or things of this sort, then we will not be able to appeal to them to get them into the Church. Because of human respect, supernatural prudence has taken a backseat and this mind set fails to understand that people convert when the doctrines of the Church are made clear to them. Faith comes through hearing, but what a person hears must be clear, otherwise, he cannot give assent to it. The rite of the Mass must have all its splendor bequeathed to it by the tradition because, insofar as it does so, it will appeal to what is noble in man and it becomes an instrument of conversion, which was often the case before the Second Vatican Council. Many people converted due to the sheer splendor, clarity and depth of the ancient liturgy.

Another sin commonly committed against prudence is the sin of negligence. Negligence according to St. Thomas implies a defect of due solicitude.[153] Many members of the Magisterium, clergy as well as others

---

[153] ST II-II, q. 54, a. 1. In ibid., a. 2, St. Thomas says that negligence is opposed to solicitude.

responsible for passing on the tradition, committed the sin of negligence because they were bound to active tradition. Instead of passing on that which was commanded to them by Christ, they either failed to do so or simply blocked it. Many parents were also guilty of negligence because of the fact that they simply presumed that the members of the Magisterium and clergy would make sure that what was necessary for their children would be passed on to them. The parents are the first educators of their children[154] and even though they should be able to rely on the Hierarchy to provide the proper education of their children, it does not take away their obligation to ensure that it is in fact being passed on to their children.

E. Sins against Justice

St. Paul says, "tradidi enim vobis, in primis quod et accepi".[155] This passage by St. Paul indicates that his primary obligation is to pass on what he received, unchanged and unadulterated. It is not the place of the person who receives the Sacred Tradition to modify and change it unless there is a sufficient reason to do so and that pertains only to those matters which can be changed. As was observed, tradition is very similar to law; each time the tradition is changed, it erodes the force of the tradition. Changing the minor traditions or the little things results psychologically in people beginning to question the bigger things, the more important things, as well as the things that cannot be changed, especially when a number of things are being changed. Because so many of the traditions have been changed within the Church, we now have generations that lack virtually any knowledge of the tradition or any concept that the tradition morally binds them. This is an injustice against the two generations that have been robbed of the Church's doctrinal, moral and disciplinary patrimony. In the last 45 years, the injustice is not just in the fact that they were robbed of these things being passed to them but even more so in the fact that they have been convinced that they do not need them.

One of the subvirtues to the virtue of justice is piety. Piety is the virtue by which one gives honor to those who are above oneself as well as care of

---

[154]See Pope St. Pius X, *An Exhortation on Catechetics to Catholic Parents and Teachers*, no. 3 (as found in *Catechism of Christian Doctrine* ordered by Pope St. Pius X, edited by Eugene Kevane, Center for Family Catechetics, Arlington, VA 1980). See also Vatican II, *Declaration on Christian Education*, no. 3; Pius XI's encyclical letter *Divini Illius Magistri*, 1, p. 59ff., encyclical letter *Mit Brennender Sorge*, March 14, 1937: A.A.S. 29 and Pius XII's allocution to the first national congress of the Italian Catholic Teachers' Association, Sept. 8, 1946: *Discourses and Radio Messages*, vol. 8, p. 218.

[155]I Cor. 15: 3: I have passed on to you, first what I also received.

those who are entrusted to a person.[156] Refusal to follow the tradition or rejection of the tradition, as we saw in how the monuments of the Church were stripped with impunity in the last two generations, is rooted in impiety. It is against piety to constantly change everything, because it is a rejection of the work of our forefathers. They labored to build the monuments, to gain greater doctrinal clarity, to perfect the discipline of the Church as well as a whole host of other things. They passed on the tradition intact which was given to them and then they added to the tradition things which would make it easier for us to understand the tradition, accept it and practice it. By the rejection and extensive overhauling of what was passed to them, the last two generations have in effect rejected their forefathers and what they bequeathed to them. It shows an unwillingness to submit one's will to what is passed on to him. The fact that they gutted churches (sometimes called "wreckovation") was a sign that they had little or no respect for those who went before them and the sacrifices they made for God and us. It is hard to see how this is not a violation of the Fourth Commandment.

It is a matter of justice not to change the tradition unless necessary due to the fact that by making an unnecessary change one deprives the baptized of those things which can aid them. A perfect example is the richness of the monuments bequeathed to us by prior generations. These monuments with all their magnificence helped those who saw them to raise their minds and hearts to God. Many of the churches being built today require such intellectual work to discern what the basic elements of the church are that it detracts from one's ability to pray. Due to the perfections of the monuments from our forefathers which aided the faithful in their spiritual lives, the gutting or destruction of these churches constituted a sin of impiety not only against our forefathers but those entrusted to their pastoral care. In fact, by all the changes to and rejection of the tradition, this has become, it is possible to say, the most unpastoral generation of ecclesiastics. By gutting the monuments, the discipline of the Church and its doctrinal clarity in its formulations and expressions, they have rendered it more difficult for those who followed them to be able to accept the tradition and to practice it faithfully.

Wholesale modifications, in the past, would have been considered, by the saints, as an act of impiety because the sweeping modifications block or deny to the subsequent generation the perfection of form of worship and the feasts of the saints that were removed. Our ancestors would have considered the constant drive to change each and every aspect of the Catholic tradition, the inability to leave any aspect of the tradition unchanged, as a sign of moral and spiritual problems and disorders. It is also impious because wholesale

---

[156]See discussion of piety beginning on page 297 in Ripperger, *Introduction to the Science of Mental Health.*

modification presumes that prior saints were not adequately directed by the Holy Spirit in the composition of the prayers of the Mass. No saint would dare to presume to affect the liturgy passed to him by his ancestors to such a degree, particularly because of the reverence he would have had regarding the guidance of past saints by the Holy Spirit. To presume to block the passing of a monument, not by perfecting it, which is actually an authentic part of the tradition, but by modifying it in such a way as to deny many of the elements in that monument is to presume that one is greater than one's ancestors. Great care has to be taken so as not to deny God's providential care of the Church manifested throughout history. In effect, such acts manifest the sin of presumption because people actually think that they are greater in knowing the mind of God than saints like Sts. Gregory the Great, Pius V, and Pius X, just to name a few.

Since the construction of these kinds of monuments is a manifestation of the devotion arising out of the charity and faith of those who constructed them, to radically modify them, without a sufficient reason, is a sin against piety. Monuments are the general patrimony of the Church under the care of specific individuals, but those specific individuals do not have the right to destroy these monuments, since they belong to the general patrimony of the Church. It is not their property. Such destruction is a kind of robbery in which subsequent generations are robbed of monuments which would ennoble their spirit and lift their minds and hearts to God. It is a kind of robbery of God, who deserves worship in suitably appointed churches. Monuments of this sort strengthen the faith of those who see them and instruct them in the teachings of the Church by the various statues and saints depicted there.

F. The Virtue of Religion

Under the virtue of justice is also the virtue of religion. Religion is the virtue by which one renders due worship to God.[157] Since the liturgies of the past were begun by our Lord and the Apostles and slowly fashioned over the course of centuries by saints, we can be assured that by worshiping according to the traditional rites, we will be worshiping God in a manner that is correct or at least that it does not offend a Him in any way. Whereas when the liturgy undergoes major changes as a departure from the tradition, it is hard to ensure that those changes are in congruity with traditional principles, principles which we have received from the Fathers and saints of the Church. In this sense, we cannot be assured that we will worship correctly if we depart from traditional principle and we may even say that we will more than likely *not* worship correctly if we deviate from the tradition. By following the tradition we safeguard our being able to follow the First Commandment which orders us to

---

[157] See ST II-II, q. 81.

give due and proper worship to God. Any deviation from the tradition that is not rooted in traditional principles runs the risk of violating the First Commandment. The First Commandment is there to ensure that we render due worship to God and since worship falls under justice, it is there to ensure that we fulfill our obligations in justice to God. Deviation from the tradition runs the risk of committing injustice against God.

Furthermore, the stripping of religious symbolism from liturgical items reduces the beauty, splendor, and mystery of the various rites of the Church. This has had a direct impact on the laity and their spiritual lives, insofar as this stripping of the monuments has lessened the various mysteries in the minds of the laity and so they tend to treat liturgical items with less reverence. In fact, they tend to treat them with a bit too much familiarity. Out of reverence for this sacred action of tradition and for those who had the faith and performed this action, insofar as they are instruments of God, we must treat their remains, their works, i.e. the monuments that they begot with great respect. Rejection of the tradition is an insult against the generations which passed on the tradition faithfully and respectfully to us.

G. Sins against Wisdom, Knowledge and Understanding

When novelty arises, confusion ensues. One of the effects of novelty or heresy is that it tends to confuse the faithful rather than to clarify what the Church has always believed. Authentic development of doctrine always provides a clearer understanding of the constant teaching of the Church. Novelty does not. But here we see that lack of adherence to the tradition leads us to act against the intellectual virtues of wisdom, knowledge and understanding. Understanding is the gift of the Holy Spirit by which we intuitively grasp the truths of faith.[158] When we reject the tradition which passes on the object of the tradition which is the truth of revelation, we cannot have an intuitive grasp of those truths. Knowledge is the gift of the Holy Spirit by which we grasp the created order the way in which God sees that order, part of which are the truths that are revealed. Again, if we reject the tradition which passes on those truths, we will not have a grasp of those truths the way that God sees them. Wisdom is the gift of the Holy Spirit by which we grasp the things that pertain to God the way that God sees them. Since the truths of revelation are passed on in the tradition, a rejection of tradition will result in foolishness, which is the vice contrary to wisdom.

---

[158]For further information, see Ripperger, *Introduction to the Science of Mental Health*, p 403.

Conclusion

We have only touched upon some of the sins committed when one rejects the tradition. By inversion we can see that if a person does not accept the Sacred Tradition as a whole, he runs the risk of losing his eternal salvation. Acceptance of the tradition has a moral as well as an intellectual binding force (the degree of which is proportionate to the nature of the thing being passed on by the tradition) on all of the members of Christ's faithful, including all members of the Magisterium and clergy. For this reason, the lay faithful have a right to expect as well as to demand that the leaders of the Church adhere perfectly to the tradition.

Bibliography

Agius, George. *Tradition and the Church.* (The Stratford Company, Boston, 1928).

Ante-Nicene Fathers [henceforth ANF – Hendrickson Publishers. Peabody, Massachusetts. 2004.]

Attwater, Donald. *A Catholic Dictionary.* The McMillan Company. NewYork. 1941.

Bernardi, Peter J. "Maurice Blondel and the Renewal of the Nature/Grace Relationship." *Communio.*

Billot, Ludovico. *De Immutabilitate Traditionis contra Modernam Hæresim Evolutionismi.* Apud Aedes Universitatis Gregorianae. Roma. 1929.

Catechism of the Catholic Church. editio typica. Libreria Editrice Vatican. 1997.

Catechismus Catholicae Ecclesiae. Editio typica. Libreria Editrice. Vaticana. 1997.

Catholic Encyclopedia. The Gilmary Society, New York, 1913.

Catholic Encyclopedic Dictionary. The Gilmary Society. New York. 1941.

Code of Canon Law Annotated. E. Cparros, M. Thériault and J. Thorn., ed. Wilson & Lafleur Limitée. Montreal. 1993.

Collectanea S. Congregationis de Propaganda Fidei seu Decreta Instructiones Rescripta pro Apostolicis Missionibus. Ex Typographia Polyglotta. Roma. 1907.

Congar, Yves. *Tradition and Traditions.* Burns and Oates., Ltd. London. 1966.

-----------------. *Meaning of Tradition.* Ignatius Press. San Francisco. 2004.

Ferrara, Christopher A. and Woods, Thomas A., Jr. *The Great Facade: Vatican II and the Regime of Novelty in the Roman Catholic Church.* Remnant Press. Wyoming, Minnesota. 2002.

Franzelin, Ioannes. *Tractatus de Divina Traditione et Scriptura.* Ex Typographia Polyglotta. Roma. 1896.

Gannon, P.J. *The Rule of Faith: Scripture and Tradition.* The Catholic Truth Society of Ireland. Dublin. 1946.

Nicene and Post-Nicene Fathers. Hendrickson Publishers. Peabody, Massachusetts. 2004.

Ott, Ludwig Ott. *Fundamentals of Catholic Dogma.* TAN Books and Publishers. Rockford, Illinois. 1974.

Pius X, Pope St. *An Exhortation on Catechetics to Catholic Parents and Teachers.* As found in *Catechism of Christian Doctrine.* Eugene Kevane, ed. Center for Family Catechetics. Arlington, VA. 1980.

-------------------. *Pascendi Dominici Gregis.* 1907.

Pius XII, Pope *Humanae Generis. 1950.*

Rahner, Karl. *Sacra Scrittura e Teologia* in *Nouvi Saggi I.* Ed. Paoline. Roma. 1968.

----------------. *Foundations of Christian Faith: An Introduction to the Idea of*

Christianity. The Seabury Press. New York. 1978.

Ratzinger, Joseph. *Revelation and Tradition.* Burns and Oats, Ltd. London. 1966.

Siri, Joseph Cardinal, *Gethsemani: Reflections on the Contemporary Theological Movement.* Franciscan Herald Press. Chicago. 1981.

The Catechism of the Council of Trent. TAN Books and Publishers, Inc. Rockford, Illinois. 1982.

The Catholic Encyclopedia. The Encyclopedia Press, Inc. The Gilmary Society. New York. 1913.

Thomas Aquinas. *Thomae Aquinatis Opera Omnia.* Issu Impensaque Leonis XIII. edita, Roma: ex Typographia Polyglotta et al. 1882.

Vincent of Lerins, *Commonitorium.* Migne. Patrologia Latina.

Wuellner, Bernard. *A Dictionary of Scholastic Philosophy.* Milwaukee: The Bruce Publishing Company. 1966.

----------------------. *Summary of Scholastic Principles.* Loyola University Press. Chicago. 1956.

Made in the USA
Coppell, TX
16 August 2023

20447095R00038